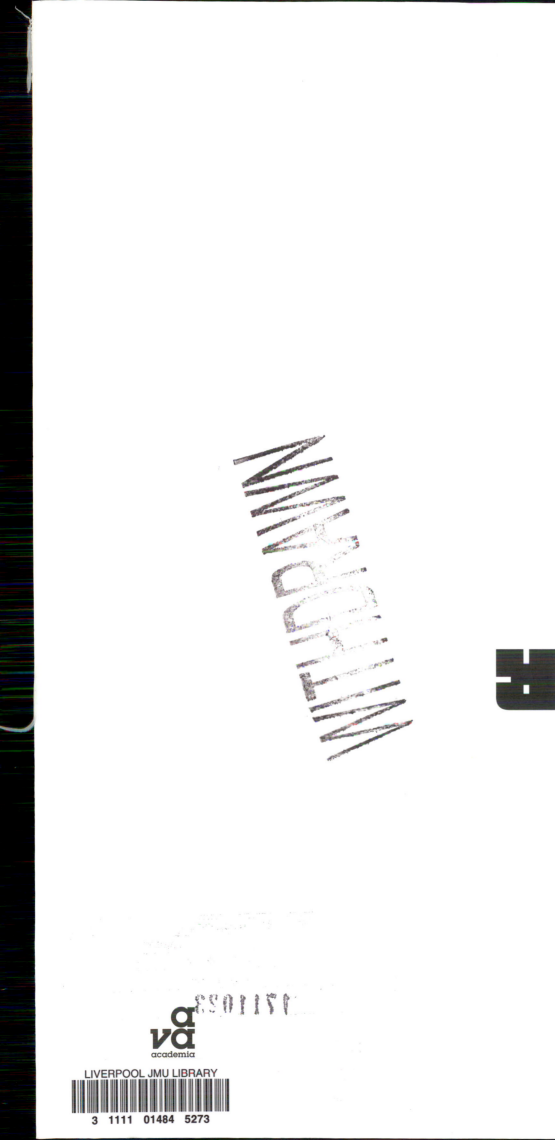

Required Reading Range
Course Reader

va
academia

An AVA Book

Published by AVA Publishing
50 Bedford Square
London
WC1B 3DP
Tel: +44 0207 631 5600
Email: enquiries@avabooks.com

Distributed by Thames & Hudson (ex-North America)
181a High Holborn
London WC1V 7QX
United Kingdom
Tel: +44 20 7845 5000
Fax: +44 20 7845 5055
Email: sales@thameshudson.co.uk
www.thamesandhudson.com

Distributed in the USA & Canada by Macmillan
Orders:
MPS
P.O. Box 470
Gordonsville, VA 22942-8501
Phone : 888-330-8477
Fax: 800-672-2054
Email: orders@mpsvirginia.com

Returns:
MPS Returns Center
14301 Litchfield Drive
Orange, VA22960
Phone: 888-330-8477

ISBN 978-2-940411-71-9

Library of Congress Cataloging-in-Publication Data
Dieffenbacher, Fiona.
Fashion Thinking: Creative approaches to the
design process / Fiona Dieffenbacher p. cm.
Includes bibliographical references and index.
ISBN: 9782940411719 (pbk. :alk. paper)
eISBN: 9782940447602
1. Fashion design. 2. Fashion -- Philosophy.
TT508 .D544 2013

10 9 8 7 6 5 4 3 2 1

Design: an Atelier project, www.atelier.ie

Production by BMAG Production Mgt. LLP, Singapore
Email: alicegoh@bmag.com.sg

FASHION THINKING

Required Reading Range
Course Reader

Fiona Dieffenbacher

Ethical: awareness/ reflection/ debate

academia

PART I **Idea** **16**

Foreword
by Shelley Fox

In the fashion industry, designers are continually looking for the *'next'*, and this book attempts to illuminate how that *'next'* might be realized, demonstrating that there is no right or wrong method of working. It seeks to understand the creative design process – how research plays a role in forming the individual design identity and offering a useful window into a fashion designer's creative thinking. The book serves to give the reader a greater understanding of why primary research is fundamental in developing a personal identity.

The interviews serve to uncover some of the often veiled or presumptive ideas of how research occurs. This understanding can only come from those who do it and who know it instinctively. The case studies also serve to articulate the fundamental need for primary research, and this is evidenced by the traceable threads of the personal design identities portrayed within the book.

Within the global fashion education system, design research is a necessary tool. With an investment in ideas at its core, it enables a student to build on their knowledge and practice. The actual doing of craft or thinking through of ideas are all valuable, and form a personal system of designing within the parameters of modern fashion practice.

Of course not all research has an obvious conclusive outcome, but it is important to understand that it is never a wasted undertaking, but training the eye to see not just look, being intuitive and reflective.

The nature of my own design practice and research process has now moved seamlessly into my own teaching approach and I have never seen the two as mutually exclusive. Designers must be open to all ways of working in order to sustain themselves as future creative thinkers.

As a self-employed fashion designer working within my own business structure and crafting my own vision throughout, it is important to note that my work has always been grounded in a strong and substantive research base. I have always believed in the pursuit of innovative methods of fabric development for structuring a personal design identity from within what is a very congested industry.

I recommend this book as an enlightening addition to the understanding and intellectual fencing in of areas of fashion research, understanding what it *could* be as a source for both the individual and larger fashion community.

1
Fashion at Belsay, 2004
Photographer: Keith Paisley.

FASH

THIN

C on

'I'm shifting between structure and chaos all the time in my process.'
Iris Van Herpen

text

Context
Introduction

An introduction to process

There will always be something enigmatic about the fashion design process itself. Despite the immediate access to fashion shows via innumerable online sites and blogs, complete with behind the scenes footage, it often appears mysterious – as if those in the inner circle are privy to an intimate secret and the outsider remains merely a voyeur to the spectacle that seems to suggest a collective, subconscious zeitgeist.

Images of designers sketching, selecting fabric, draping and fitting a model are all too familiar. Indeed, these steps are at the very core of the design experience. But the more intimate process that speaks to how the designer has developed their own particular approach and thinking has largely gone undocumented.

Not everyone begins with a sketch; indeed some don't sketch at all (Donna Karan and Isabel Toledo are only two such examples), preferring to begin with fabric or work via flat pattern or 3D draping methods. No two processes are exactly the same. Every designer will yield varying results due to their personal design philosophy and aesthetic.

It is exactly this diversity of approach to fashion thinking that this book seeks to capture. By doing so, it will highlight the variety of distinctive methods of working versus heralding one traditional approach as being the only road map for the journey.

Other texts on the subject offer a 'one size fits all' ordering of the steps within the design process: Research – sketch – flat-pattern/drape – fabrication – make. While this order works for many designers in the field and these steps are essential building blocks of a functional design process, this ordering is not the only approach. Designers should co-opt or upend this process for themselves, driven by their own particular perspective and instinct.

Perhaps it is best to suggest that design happens in any order that works for you – you being the only constant within the process. You alone dictate how you begin, how you develop and how you resolve that process through to its final conclusion.

Unmasking the design process is not as easy as it might appear, nor is it something that designers are keen to engage in. It is, however, necessary to investigate and to present examples of a variety of approaches in order for emerging designers to discover their own by comparison.

This book follows nine student designers, documenting their responses to a variety of design briefs and the thought process that follows through the three stages of Idea, Concept and Design. For the purposes of this text we are focused solely on the ideation stage of these projects, some resulting in 2D outcomes and others in 3D collections.

Hopefully it won't be a case of the Emperor's New Clothes and in unmasking the process we will discover that he's not in fact naked, but rather fully clothed in a garb of intentionality and a series of decisions that reveal a never-ending creative process.

There is no 'right' way to approach design; there are no 'wrong' turns. Everything matters. Designers are problem-solvers. Problems present challenges that require solutions and these often lead to the most original design, or at least one the designer hadn't thought of initially. Mistakes must also be embraced for they often lead to the most glorious discoveries that one could not have predicted, yielding fresh concepts that drive silhouette and form forward. Innovation often happens on the heels of error in the midst of chaos and complexity.

Fashion thinking involves harnessing the vast array of skills at the designer's disposal, while embracing the chaos of the process itself. This might include upending traditional approaches or reappropriating them to unearth new ways of creating and making clothes.

Design is a journey of an undetermined number of steps. As the projects in this book demonstrate, there are multiple entry points into that process and a million ways out. In between, there are some consistent doors that each designer will go through (albeit in a different order) and there are consistent tools they will utilize to accomplish the end result, but the rest is up for grabs.

Challenging the status quo

Across the decades and within many spheres of influence, iconic change-makers arise to challenge the way things have been done historically or traditionally within their fields. Some take traditional techniques and upend them (McQueen/Savile Row tailoring), and some radically redefine the genre itself (Comme des Garçons/Maison Martin Margiela).

Innovators aren't swayed by the tide of popular opinion; they enter into new territory without fear because they have a vision of something as yet unseen by others. This is true of designers as well as any other change-maker.

Looking back through fashion history, many iconic designers challenged the status quo, shaped culture and impacted society as a result. Each decade saw distinct shifts and key leaders responsible for them. In the 1920s , for example, Gabrielle 'Coco' Chanel revolutionized fashion by utilizing modest fabrics such as jersey knits for day wear, combining comfort and style. In the 1930s, Elsa Schiaparelli brought fashion and art together by collaborating with the surrealist Salvador Dali. Decades later, Vivienne Westwood and Malcolm McLaren combined fashion and music and are credited with launching the ant-Establishment Punk movement of the seventies. Innovators simultaneously reflect and challenge culture. Fashion sits centre stage in this role, as designers tap into the collective zeitgeist and trends emerge influencing our subconcious choices in ways we often aren't aware of.

The main question to be asked of fashion education today is, 'Are we training students to design clothes or to create fashion? To be makers or creators, or both?' If we are training students to understand the difference between these two spheres and what it means to truly create fashion, we need to encourage design thinking as a method of envisioning a reality that does not yet exist. Then we will see a real shift towards innovation. But if we are only training students to design clothes via a process that is rote and mundane, then we've missed the point entirely.

Establishing frameworks

Frameworks exist everywhere – some are more apparent than others. The keys on a piano, for example, provide the structure and limitations necessary for a musician to create music. Our own central nervous system allows us the luxury to think, act and live freely. Creativity then, it could be argued, can best function when set free within a framework (or system).

New fashion systems arise out of individually developed approaches to the design process itself. We create these subconsciously – and a seasoned designer moves through the process instinctively, often not realizing why or how they are doing so because the process itself is so innate.

The design cycle

In this book we will follow nine projects, step-by-step through the three stages of 'Idea', 'Concept' and 'Design', in the hope that by seeing the thought processes of other designers, this will enable students to recognize their own approach.

The designer enters the cycle at any given point and works through it in their own way. They work in a succession of varying sequences, producing different outcomes at each stage, moving ideas forward or mapping back and forth continuously. The entry point itself can be identified by assessing a typical approach to design. For example, if a student naturally gravitates to expressing their initial design ideas via textile development or 3D draping, this should be the entry point into the design process (or cycle).

Many students struggle to understand their process. Very few reflect on their method of working or seek to understand why they did what they did. For the purposes of this book, we will identify two umbrella systems under which a variety of methods might be grouped. This should enable students to better understand their own methods of working.

Linear vs Random Process

Many students simply have a natural working method that produces good results with little effort. Others are still evolving their style and design sensibilities and need the tangible structure of a framework to help them get the most out of their ideas.

The 'Linear Framework' builds one idea upon another in a coherent way to form a concept. Design occurs in a sequential fashion; each design idea is derived from the last and so on. In this process, themes are easily detected as they arise. This may include brainstorming, mind-mapping, journaling, note taking and creating lists that seek to organize initial ideas into elements and move them forward into useable parts. There is a sense of order to the process.

The 'Random Framework' develops scattered design ideas and thoughts at will, with no apparent order. These then require assessment to identify common connections [random process]. In this case, it is essential to constantly assess and edit, asking what works best and intentionally looking for correlation. The designer selects key ideas and develops variations from these edits to achieve a cohesive concept.

Both require intentionality at some point within the process. Both require designers to take ownership of not only their ideas, but also the process itself. By understanding their approach they will learn to become independent thinkers and make connections within the various spheres of design at an early stage in their development as a designer.

Both these frameworks merely serve as tools to enable the beginning designer to recognize how they work and, as a result, to better reflect on their own process as they move through it. By doing so they become more self-aware along the way, and as a result will become more astute designers.

But it is important to remember that the starting point only indicates the entry to the journey – not the final destination. A successful collection is derived from a multi-faceted journey of discovery and reflection.

LINEAR THINKING

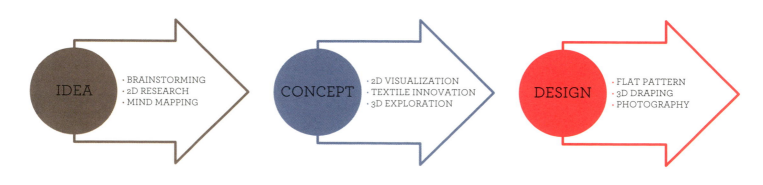

IDEA
- BRAINSTORMING
- 2D RESEARCH
- MIND MAPPING

CONCEPT
- 2D VISUALIZATION
- TEXTILE INNOVATION
- 3D EXPLORATION

DESIGN
- FLAT PATTERN
- 3D DRAPING
- PHOTOGRAPHY

RANDOM PROCESS

THE DESIGN CYCLE

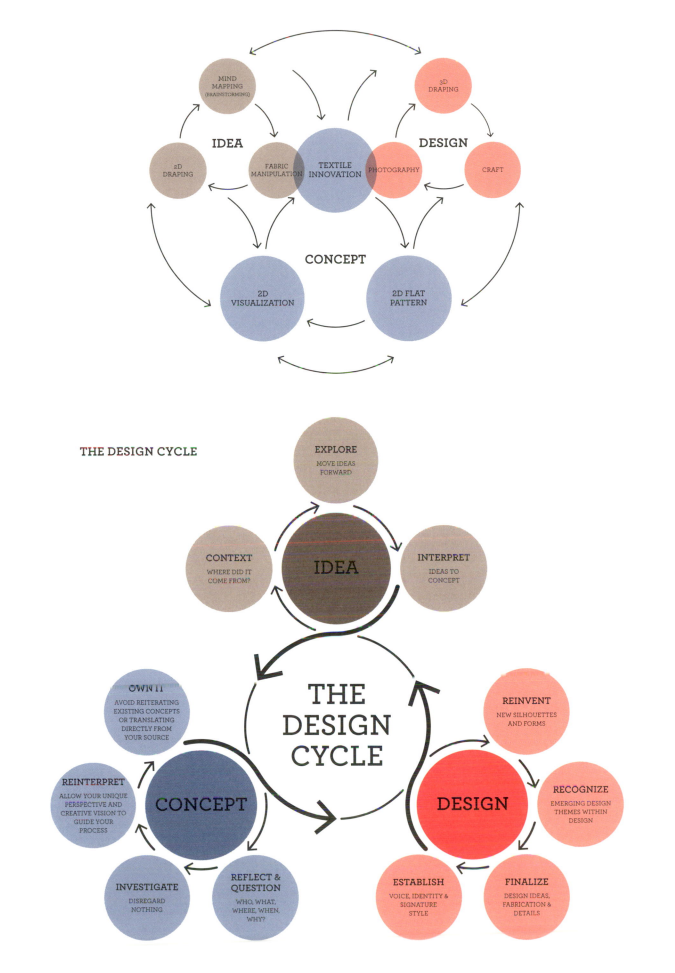

Context
How to get the most out of this book

This book is split into three parts: Idea, Concept and Design. Within each part, we view fashion design through four lenses:

Process Process pages introduce each of the three stages and remind us of where we are in the design cycle.

Practice Practice pages form the basis of the book, and look at nine real-life student projects.

Perspective Perspective pages offer the thoughts of academics and established fashion designers.

Point of View Point of View pages offer the thoughts of practitioners working across all areas of the fashion world.

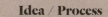

Process

A diagram indicates where in the process the individual stages come.

The stage is introduced with a definition and discussion.

Practice

Nine student projects make up these sections. Each project begins with a brief synopsis and a list of the key processes used at each stage in the process.

The projects are illustrated with real-life images and supported by accompanying captions.

Perspective

Academics and established fashion designers offer their thoughts on the thinking behind fashion design.

Point of View

Practitioners from a range of backgrounds in the fashion industry offer their thoughts on process and innovation.

FASHI

THINK

PART I

Idea

'Fashion is not something that exists in dresses only. Fashion is in the sky, in the street, fashion has to do with ideas, the way we live, what is happening.'

Coco Chanel

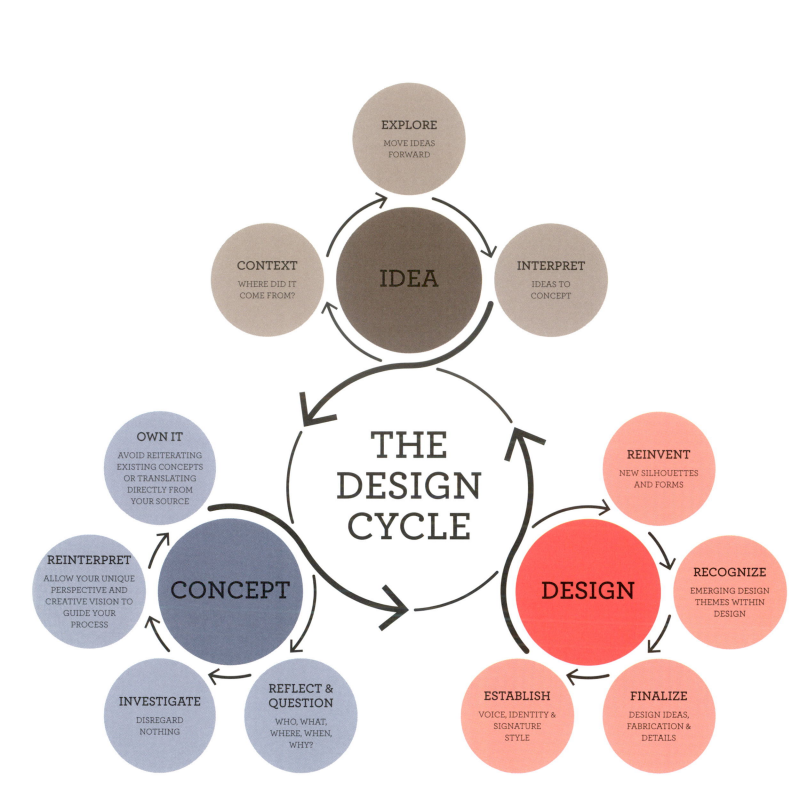

THE DESIGN CYCLE

IDEA

EXPLORE
MOVE IDEAS FORWARD

CONTEXT
WHERE DID IT COME FROM?

INTERPRET
IDEAS TO CONCEPT

CONCEPT

OWN IT
AVOID REITERATING EXISTING CONCEPTS OR TRANSLATING DIRECTLY FROM YOUR SOURCE

REINTERPRET
ALLOW YOUR UNIQUE PERSPECTIVE AND CREATIVE VISION TO GUIDE YOUR PROCESS

INVESTIGATE
DISREGARD NOTHING

REFLECT & QUESTION
WHO, WHAT, WHERE, WHEN, WHY?

DESIGN

REINVENT
NEW SILHOUETTES AND FORMS

RECOGNIZE
EMERGING DESIGN THEMES WITHIN DESIGN

FINALIZE
DESIGN IDEAS, FABRICATION & DETAILS

ESTABLISH
VOICE, IDENTITY & SIGNATURE STYLE

Idea / Process

idea:
— a personal opinion or belief
— a thought to be presented as a suggestion
— an impression or knowledge of something
— a concept that exists in the mind only
— a mental image that reflects reality

An idea is the catalyst that begins any project. The origin of the word comes from late Middle English via Latin from the Greek *idea*, from the base of *idein* 'to see' therefore at its very core it can be described as a way of seeing. In this first stage, the designer grapples with their imagination in order to bring the idea into reality, into a recognizable form. In the context of fashion design, what is inexplicable becomes tangible within the design process itself and in the final expression of clothing.

Finding the right idea is one thing but moving it forward and investigating all the options is also important in order to push yourself into new territory. How you choose to move towards that next step is significant, as this reveals your own particular way of working and approach to design. This is often intuitive but can be further articulated and refined with self-reflection on your own process throughout each stage.

Design students must approach the unpacking of an idea with the willingness to engage fully in the process of primary (first-hand) research at the onset of a project. This can include first-hand experience (personal memory, life experiences), taking photographs, conducting interviews along with other means of data-collection. With the help of the Internet, one can amass a wide range of information and imagery in a matter of minutes to support the initial idea, but this approach should be viewed as a supportive research method and not as the sole means of investigation at this early stage of your process.

Any idea in the right hands can be moved forward into a plausible concept and subsequently a tangible reality when harnessing design thinking. The fashion design team of Rodarte provides us with a good example. '[Their] ideation process represents a chaotic mash of conversations and references, taking inspiration from such disparate themes such as: Horror movies, Renaissance Painting and opera. Ideas, half-ideas, fleeting notions are bubbling in their minds constantly. But, in fact, these seemingly random topics of conversation are their memories and their lifeblood, and the very foundation of their work.'[1]

Rodarte's working method reflects an organic process that responds to the environment around them, driven by their own particular set of interests in the world. Their work is instinctual, authentic and uncensored, which is true of any true visionary. An ideation process that is intensely personal produces the best results.

1. 'The Rodarte Effect' by Evgenia Peretz, *Vanity Fair*, USA, March 2012

An investigation into movement and dance, using zero-waste and sustainable methods.

Process

Brainstorming / free association	Textile / knit development	3D draping and construction
Mind mapping	Zero-waste flat pattern	Fabric manipulation
Music / Dance	2D sketching	Zero-waste cutting
Video	3D draping	Textile innovation
2D painting	Surface textile design	Ethics
Photography	Self-editing	Sustainable practice
Doodling	Recycling	
Surface print design		

Hope for the Future

Janelle Abbott

This was Janelle's final project within her 'Concepts' course during her third year of study in pursuit of her BFA degree in Fashion Design at Parsons The New School for Design.

Students were asked to design a collection initially incubated within a practice of **'mind mapping'**. They were asked to develop initial ideas for a ten- to fifteen-look collection.

The mind-mapping process is one that starts with a small segment of collected inspiration – a song, a lyric, a poem, or a picture. Once the source is obtained, it is pondered and, through whatever medium the designer chooses, documented until a point 'a' is reached. Original media then leads the designer through points 'b', 'c', 'd', 'e' and so on, to a moment of self-revelation, enlightenment and true inspiration – a point at which the design process is fully ready to begin. In the case of this particular assignment, the class was instructed to incubate ideas from explicit media (lyrical, verbal, written, and moving image, for example).

Where did the idea come from?

Janelle's project began when her instructor played a song in class, and then asked the students to create a mind-map to reflect the song. This was a simple exercise to ignite an idea in each student that would direct their own individual mind-mapping process.

Initially, this action of mapping manifested itself within Janelle's process apart from fashion. She was more interested in connecting the action of dancing to drawing than in designing clothing. But as the work progressed, it became increasingly clear how this chain of practices – dance, drawing, fashion – all combined together in a shared understanding of motion. From her initial idea, she had now identified the overarching theme that would inform her process.

The method of mind-mapping pushed Janelle beyond prescribed conceptions and notions, and in this way, it was perhaps beneficial to her process that considerations of clothing not be impacted. Beginning from an outside-in perspective, her process of investigation in the realms of music, dance and drawing provided questioning points that informed how she approached fashion design and clothing in a new way.

Janelle's lifelong relationship with dance provided the starting point for her initial idea for this project. She had taken dance classes throughout her youth, and this had created something of a love/hate relationship with the medium. As a child, the car-ride to the studio would often be spent dreading the lesson ahead, but once her hand was on the barre, that would all disappear and she would remember all that she loved most about the discipline.

After moving to New York City, Janelle abandoned dance as a formal practice. However, she continued informally, performing only for her camera in various classrooms on campus.

Inspired by an instructor who himself was interested in the connections to be made between drawing and dance, she began to investigate this concept further. She found that, as a medium, dance allowed her to detach a small portion of her mind from consciousness and allow the remaining portion to 'ignite' with ideas.

She began to make new connections within the context of dance and fashion: the idea of 'reviving the flattened "body" of fashion; to move, activate, and engage it', became the driving force behind her idea.

Janelle's first step in the creative process for this project began with her listening to Sufjan Stevens' *Impossible Soul* one night while sitting on her bedroom floor. Halfway into the song she started painting on mint green paper with white acrylic and ink. As a result of this process, she developed four distinctive brush strokes. A few days later, in an empty classroom, she played the soundtrack again and began investigating the brush strokes one by one; drawing them on the board in chalk, then dancing to the song in a manner that mimicked each stroke, first wearing restrictive clothing, then a second time with oversized, 'flowing' clothing.

Using a personal experience to inform the design process provides authenticity that leads to original concepts, which have ownership from the beginning. Here, Janelle not only made connections from something extremely personal, but by bringing dance into the context of design she allowed this to impact on the disciplines of drawing and fashion in new ways, and therefore created a new personal approach to design itself.

1 / 2 / 3
Brush stroke images
Janelle used brush strokes to make connections between the acts of drawing and dancing. These would later be used to inform the silhouette, form and surface design of her collection.

Moving ideas forward

Between the time Janelle developed the brush strokes and made the connections between the acts of drawing and dancing, she also began to drape 3D shapes in heavyweight wool, working on a process of doubling fabric back on itself, mimicking the various components of the brush strokes.

Janelle was searching for a way to connect drawing more directly to fashion through the lens of dance, without explicitly referencing the action. She wanted the fabric to 'dance' across the dress form in the same manner that she had danced across the empty classroom. 'The drapes that I developed were apart from the initial concept, but at the same time in tune with its sentiment because they sought to capture movement in motion. The weight of the wool retained shapes as I rolled the fabric diagonally and horizontally across the dress form, creating ripples and recessions like the imprint of waves on sand. I photographed this series and used several of the drapes later to develop my final sketches. In order to make this segment of my process (seemingly detached from a direct relationship to the drawing/dancing section of the project) more contextualized, I combined ideas and resolutions obtained through those portions of this project. In this manner, stepping away from a strictly conceived series of events helped to create a more enigmatic collection; many things were linear, but at the same time, a selection of things appeared abrupt yet also transitional.'

Janelle's particular process of exploration is chaotic and random but also embraces error as a useful tool within the process: 'I will use any excuse to be a mess, to be rowdy, to be constantly in motion. The period of exploration that this particular project embarked on was one that had strict guidelines and no limits. Everything was permissible but not everything, in the end, was presentable.'

Janelle videotaped herself throughout the initial process and began utilizing the still shots from the videos to create drapes based on how the clothing looked captured in space. Her goal was to create clothing that looked as if it was in motion while remaining static on the body.

4 / 5 / 6

Video footage of movement and dance

Janelle used videos of herself dancing to observe how the clothing looked in movement. She then used this footage to help create drapes.

Idea to concept

Janelle listened to the song a second time in class and doodled on paper bags; from here, she developed four more strokes that she was interested in using as a starting point to create original prints and patterns.

For Janelle, the idea of connecting drawing to dance, and, by extension, connecting music to drawing to dance to fashion, was one that manifested within the work through silhouette and form, but also via surface design and aesthetics. Through embroidery, hand painting and hand-knits, she integrated into the garments the brush strokes that had been developed in the very first stage of her process – a blatant representation of the process of mind-mapping, but an abstract reference to the initially investigated song. In the same way, the manner in which the dance/drapes were captured within each garment also teetered on the edge of obvious with the best of intentions.

Janelle utilized the method of mind-mapping in a variety of ways throughout the various stages of design; in its most recognizable form in micro ways and also within the 3D draping process in macro terms.

'Each week we would have an assignment due, specific to each student's project and the shape their process was taking. Each assignment related to one another in the manner that one builds a puzzle, mapping out the edges first (so that the framework is clear), then collecting the interior pieces together until an image is revealed. My instructor was very open to my personal interpretation of what each assignment might entail, so I would come to class with whatever it was that I had come up with that week. More often than not, I would have in hand a resolution to resign and quit, along with a stack of doodles and a few new developments on surface designs and textile manipulations.

After the mind-mapping (music listening, drawing, dancing/draping) was completed, I began to work with the stills collected from the dance pieces by scratching ideas onto croquis figures that I had photocopied several times over. Referring each piece to a similar figure assisted me in expediting my process, but also, understanding the shape, weight, and proportion of each garment idea relative to one another. This collection of 30–40 sketches was what I handed in for my 'first assignment'.

Turn to page 84 to see PART II (Concept) of this project, or page 148 for PART III (Design).

A collection based on culture and social processes, from garment design to presentation.

Process

Observational research	2D visualization	3D construction
Narrative	Fashion cultural reference	Brainstorming
Digital technology	3D deconstruction	2D / 3D visualization
Brainstorming	2D collage	Digital technical flat drawing
2D sketching	Narrative	2D editing
Journaling	3D draping	Exhibition
Digital collage	Colour / fabrication	
Exhibition	2D flat pattern	

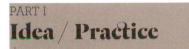

Virtual Appropriation
Melitta Baumeister

This project was undertaken as part of Melitta's BFA senior thesis collection at Pforzheim University in Germany in 2010. The collection comprised eight looks and took five months to create. It was shown to an industry panel and Melitta also created a follow-up exhibition in a public space. As a result, she was nominated for the Apolda European Design Award 2011, an award scheme aiming to support and promote promising young European designers.

Where did the idea come from?

The initial idea for this project began with an abstract thought. Melitta's collection was based on the idea that fashion can be used as a medium to understand our daily lives and to question the social behaviour of our society. Observing social processes as a starting point for research gave Melitta the opportunity to use fashion to reflect society.

Melitta began by considering the digital world as a main idea, thought, interest and inspiration. Initially, she was inspired by the theories of the French philosopher, Jean Baudrillard, where he discusses the dematerialization of the objective world by digital media. For Baudrillard, the actual reality does not disappear but the forms we know of as reality do. Space and time dissolve or undergo a profound restructuring and the earlier forms of objectively tangible reality disappear.

The principle of simulation expressed by mass media and virtual reality is a major presence in current society. Within her initial process, Melitta began to attempt to analyse these ideas. Melitta describes it as being similar to a documentary where the clothes themselves tell a story. The focus is not on the product, but more on the conceptual expression of it. She developed the idea by observing the existing virtual world and the various processes taking place within it, and looking at the use of digital technology within fashion representation.

Melitta was interested in exploring the breakdown of consent and truth between reality and the digitally presented image, which often becomes a new digitally manipulated reality: 'Pictures can be seamlessly altered, blended and mixed together, making anything possible, and creating something that does not exist in the lived-in world, something that was only imagined before: fashion and clothing in its dematerialized, artificial form; unreal garments in its representation as something that might be even closer to what we desire. Almost like an avatar – a visual self-representation of people in a digital way that communicates their identity – something that is not real in the lived-in world but represents one's interest; a "synthetic ideal"'.

1
Exploring ideas
Melitta's collection was based on the idea that fashion can be used as a medium to understand our daily lives and to question the social behaviour.

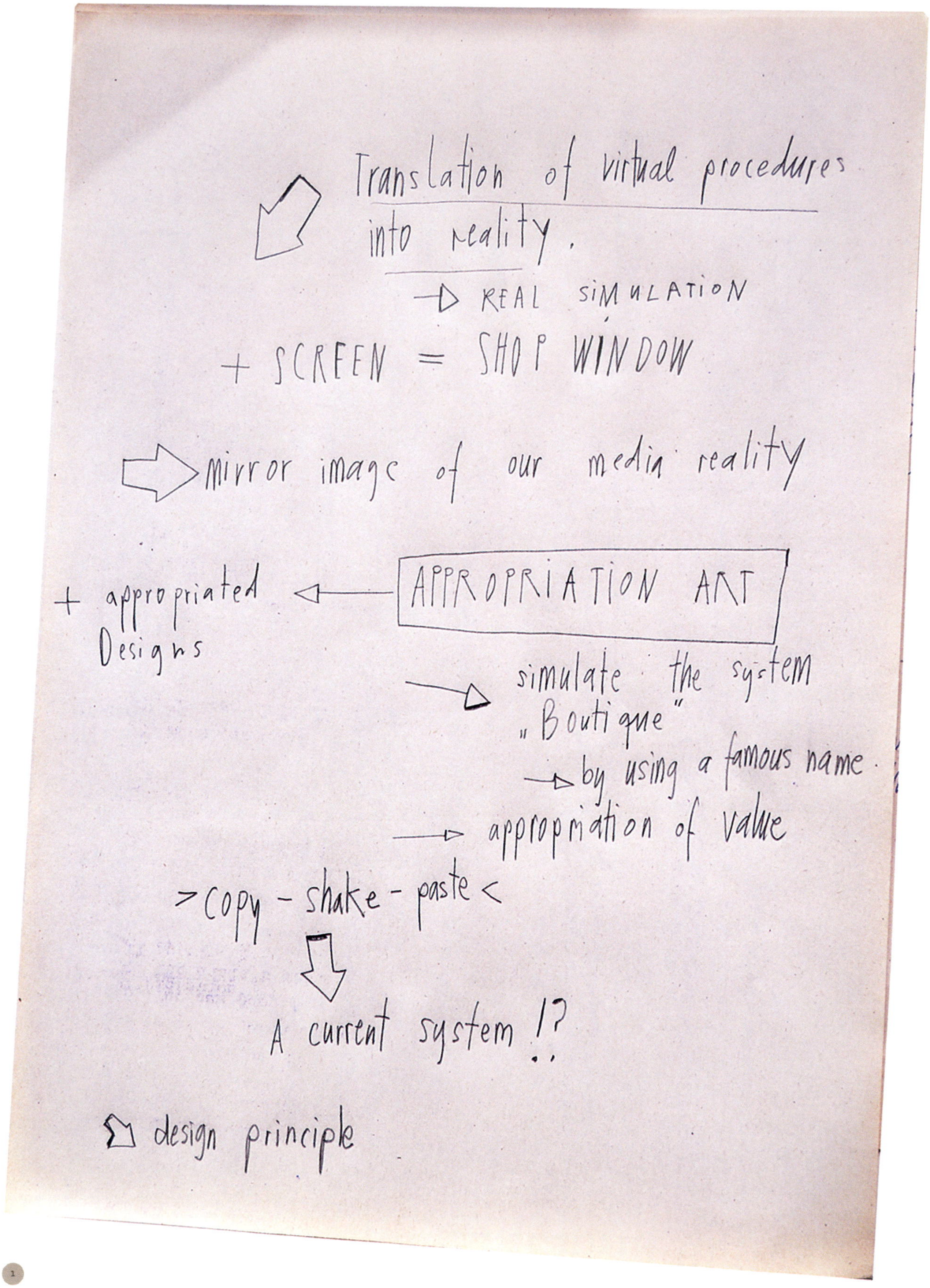

Translation of virtual procedures into reality.

→ REAL SIMULATION

+ SCREEN = SHOP WINDOW

⇒ Mirror image of our media reality

+ appropriated Designs ← APPROPRIATION ART

→ simulate the system "Boutique"

→ by using a famous name.

→ appropriation of value

>copy - shake - paste<

A current system !?..

⇨ design principle

2

Project mapping

Melitta's project looked at a variety
of methods for digital manipulation,
appropriating existing creations for
new forms.

Moving ideas forward

In order to help refine her ideas during the next phase
in the process, Melitta brainstormed and searched for
key words to describe her thoughts in relation to the
themes that arose from her earlier exploration. Here she
began to research virtual processes and discovered the
appropriation of art, which represented similarities to
the virtual world for her.

Some of the key words she used include: virtual
processes, dematerialization, simulation, loss of truth,
appropriation art, ready-made, copy/paste, collage,
aesthetics and value appropriation. Melitta used these
words as a starting point for her research along with
gathering images, which helped her to find techniques
of surface fabric manipulation to translate the idea into
a concept then into a garment. The images were also
important to create a certain mood for the collection
(colours and look) and to keep the key words and
concept in mind.

She then considered appropriation art in virtual
processes as a similar approach to digital manipulation.
She looked at a variety of actions to interpret this theme
further: for example, the 'copy/paste' action commonly
used in digital environments, and the ready-made
garment as an example of creating something new out
of existing material.

After focusing her direction, Melitta began visualizing
her ideas in mood boards and sketchbooks, using
images, words, photography and drawings. In this
case, she referenced the work of artist Egon Schiele. By
painting over his drawings, she created her own act of
appropriation art. This allowed her to understand the
process of reusing existing material through making,
rather than simply documenting.

③

VIRTUAL PROCESSES

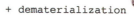

+ dematerialization

+ disembodime

+ garments are robbed
  of their function !

3 / 4 / 5

Sketchbook development

Melitta used images, words,
photography and sketches to
explore the act of appropriation art.
By painting over the work of Egon
Schiele, for example, she was able to
explore her own ideas.

④

⑤

TR AGMENT

6

Shopfront

As part of her idea process, Melitta used an empty shop window to experiment with labelling, viewing and presentation ideas.

Idea to concept

Melitta also used the principle of appropriation art for her next stage of development. She borrowed images of clothing she found on the Internet and made collages from these using Photoshop, deconstructing and adopting elements she found interesting. Using illustrations and sketches, she investigated different silhouettes. For this project she used 'ready-made' clothing and digital computer programs to create new forms. Her selection of garments (mostly menswear) was driven by her own personal aesthetic. She focused on the translation of men's jackets into womenswear.

As part of her research, Melitta viewed web pages and other simulations of reality. This gave her the idea to turn a virtual web page into a physical retail space, and this was developed further in later stages.

7

Photoshop experimentation

Melitta found images of clothes on the Internet and used these to play with new forms. Here, she tries turning men's jackets into womenswear.

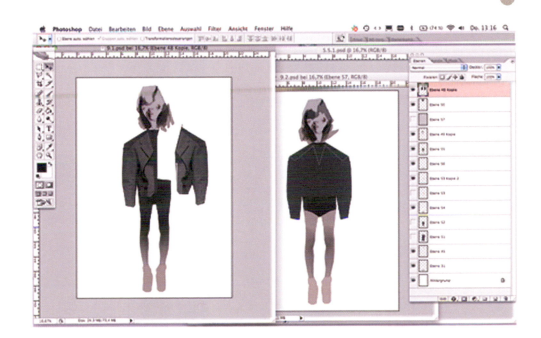

Turn to page 90 to see PART II (Concept) of this project, or page 154 for PART III (Design).

Textile innovation driven by an investigation into what lies beneath the skin.

Process

2D visualization	2D visualization	Self-reflection
Narrative	3D draping	Textile innovation
Textile exploration	2D flat pattern	3D draping
Hand craft	Printing technology	Sustainable practice
Embroidery	Textile surface design	Technology
Knitting		Collaboration
Digital technology		Hand craft
		Editorial photography

Neurovision

Jovana Mirabile

This project follows the development of Jovana Mirabile's BFA senior thesis collection, comprising six looks and a line of accessories, including bags, shoes and jewellery. This was a year-long process, culminating in a thesis review presentation to an industry panel. As a result, Jovana was nominated for 'Designer of the Year' at Parsons and the collection was showcased at the Parsons' Fashion Gala in May 2011.

Many designers have a tactile approach to design and often choose to work in this way. They typically gravitate towards the craft of 'making', often developing swatches with handcrafted techniques such as beading, embroidery and appliqué, along with textile dyeing and printing. This was Jovana's approach. The basis for this project is textile innovation, where experimentation is undertaken using a variety of existing dye, print and embellishment techniques. The process was then driven forward by individual ideas and concepts towards the final design stage.

...the basis for this project is textile innovation, where experimentation is undertaken using a variety of existing dye, print, and embellishment techniques. **Jovana Mirabile**

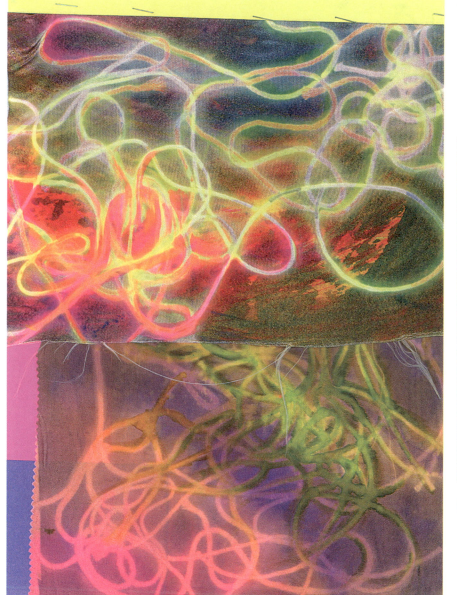

Where did the idea come from?

The project had a random beginning with no concrete idea other than the exploration of materiality. Rooted in textile development, the process began with investigating the techniques of shibori, batik, reactive and resistance dyeing and heat transfer printing. Initially free-form and experimental, and without preconceived expectations, the outcome of this initial stage of idea-making resulted in images that were reminiscent of X-rays and MRI brain scans.

1 / 2 / 3

Dyeing techniques

Jovana's initial process was rooted in textile development. While playing with shibori, discharge, rusting and heat transfer techniques, Jovana started to recognize the results as resembling body imaging scans.

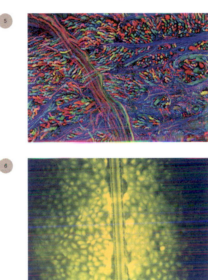

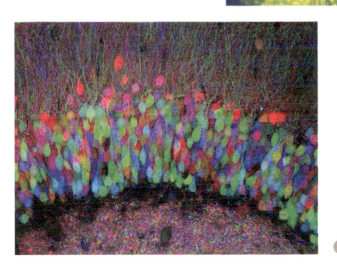

4 / 5 / 6 / 7
Body imaging
To explore these ideas further, Jovana collected a number of X-ray, MRI and PET scan images. Here we see Brainbow cell activity, fluorescent brain cells and nerve cells.

Moving ideas forward

During this next phase, the brain scan idea that had arisen from Jovana's original experimentation was further explored. This became a natural progression through the process, as more information was required in order to determine whether or not the idea had enough depth and breadth to support the design development of the collection.

Employing 2D visualization in this information-gathering stage, Jovana collected a wide variety of X-ray, MRI, and PET scan images. This led to a fascination with the technology used to see inside the human body. A narrative means of exploration was utilized in order to push these ideas forward: excerpts from the book *Metal Flesh and the Evolution of Man: Technology Takes Over* by Olliver Dyens came into play and Jovana created connections between technology and its interaction with the body. Sections of the book brought to mind the purpose of our skin, its functions, what it protects, and how we perceive it. This became a major theme and was further explored through brainstorming and creating lists of ideas. As a result, the central theme 'Internal/External' emerged: looking at our skin as the outer protective layer of our physical being as well as acting as a barrier to what lies within.

Making connections from one phase to another is important at this early stage. Jovana acted on her instincts and was led by her process. She responded to the textiles and the images they suggested and gathered more information, employing a variety of methods along the way. Had she not done so, her idea may simply have ended at the textile development stage and not advanced to a more meaningful interpretation. Now with a concrete theme to develop, 'The purpose of skin: protection from within and without', she had, from a random beginning, defined a specific direction.

Research is a multifaceted process where the designer must be willing to go on a journey of discovery, allowing each step to lead organically to the next. Many students make the mistake of believing they have to stick to their first idea and execute that precisely, without deviation. On the contrary, there should be the freedom to allow oneself to arrive somewhere entirely new. This is exactly the point of the evolution of ideas.

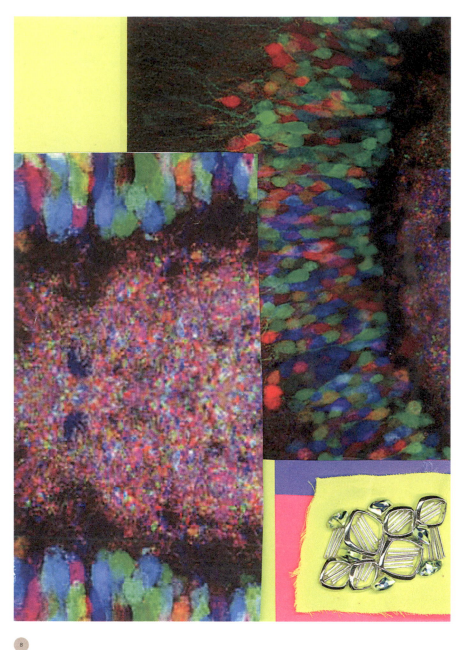

Surface techniques
Using dyeing techniques, embroidery and knitting, Jovana was able to reflect the vivid effects of the body scans.

...*overarching themes of protection and the perception of beauty arose.* Jovana Mirabile

Idea to concept

Searching for alternative interpretations surrounding the notion of skin, Jovana considered the phrase 'beauty is skin deep' and first translated it in a literal sense by looking at what lies beneath the skin. She focused on X-rays and scans of cancer cells, tumours and bacterial infections, and in so doing, while seeking to uncover the grotesque and mysterious physical matter that lies beneath the skin, discovered something she found to be organically beautiful. As a result, the overarching themes of protection and the perception of beauty arose.

With this new direction, Jovana returned to textile innovation and handcraft methods to develop original fabrications. To do this, she used dyeing techniques, embroideries and knit swatches to reflect the beauty of the vivid, acid colours created within the organic patterns of the scans and X-rays. Here, she was reapplying new methods, but this time within a new context that had been informed by her research. Selected images of cancer cells, brainwaves and X-rays were scanned along with original artwork and manipulated together to form surface prints. This use of digital technology allowed Jovana to transform 2D images into original textile designs. Through trial and error, she generated a vast amount of print designs which could then be narrowed down to four key prints that best represented the concept.

10

11

Turn to page 96 to see PART II (Concept) of this project, or page 160 for PART III (Design).

A reinvention of traditional craft techniques to create new textiles and garments.

Process

Research	Textile development	'Knitted' textile development
2D visualization	Digital technology	Materiality
Fabric manipulation	3D development	3D draping
Craft techniques	Craft technique	Photography
Textile research	3D form	Editorial direction
Materiality	2D visualization	2D visual narration
3D digital draping	Materiality	Film
Photography	Textile innovation	
Technical drawing	3D textile / draping	
3D draping		

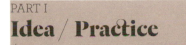

Knitting and Pleating

Jie Li

Jie Li studied at the University of Salford in Manchester, UK and obtained a BA degree in Fashion Design, focusing on womenswear. Jie continued her studies in the MFA Design and Society program at Parsons The New School for Design. This project was submitted for the McQueen Fashion Design Contest, sponsored by the Metropolitan Museum of Art and open to US students in a graduate program.

In recognition of Alexander McQueen's pivotal role in shaping millennial fashion through technique, narrative, collaboration and showmanship, graduate students were encouraged to embrace these aspects as inspiration to create garments that continued to push fashion forward. McQueen was a technical and conceptual designer influenced by art, literature, music, history, nature, science, and contemporary culture at large. Students were encouraged to continue his legacy and his masterful ability to create objects of fantasy set in spectacular catwalk presentations to articulate his vision. In addition, he was able to distil these ideas into wearable garments and build an international brand. Students were tasked with submitting entries that addressed the same parameters in the form of 2D and 3D work in two looks (one catwalk and one retail). They were then asked to select one look to be represented in a format that would effectively communicate their narrative; either in the form of printed editorial photography, short film, animation or other sensory outcomes.

Where did the idea come from?

Students were asked to research two craft techniques. As a result of her research, Jie found pleating and hand knitting to interest her the most and consequently decided to combine the two techniques to create a new craft. Jie began her research in a linear way, visiting the library and browsing the Internet to gather images to give a broad overview of visual ideas.

In the midst of her research, Jie discovered an image by the artist Lydia Hirte, who created paper 'drawings' or paper manipulations, including pleats. This singular image and the artist's method of working inspired Jie, as the shapes created were reminiscent of the loops of knitwear. She decided to apply this technique to the context of craft and began working with cut paper to recreate techniques that were reminiscent of these pleats and knit-like forms.

Jie did not know how to knit and in this particular instance this was a distinct advantage as she approached this craft from a completely different perspective. First, she looked at diagrams of the basic knit stitch. She enlarged these to show the loops clearly and followed the pattern visually but instead of using yarn, she created strips of pleated woven fabric, thus combining pleating and knitting.

Moving ideas forward

Jie collected pictures of stitch formations and pleats from basic-level handcraft magazines and books, and watched YouTube videos to learn how to knit. She also did additional research about art handcrafts – specifically paper manipulation – and considered which methods would work the best. Not only was Jie applying the art of knitting within a new context by using pleated fabric instead of yarn, she was also taking the knit stitch into a woven realm by following the motion and technique of 'knitting' by using her hands to pull the woven strips in and out of the loops.

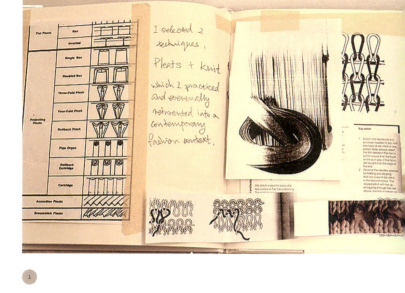

1

2

1

Inspiration pages
Jie discovered the work of artist Lydia Hirte, who creates paper 'drawings' and manipulations. She decided to apply some of her techniques to her own work with knitwear.

2

Fabric samples
A number of effects can be achieved through pleating, looping and folding fabric.

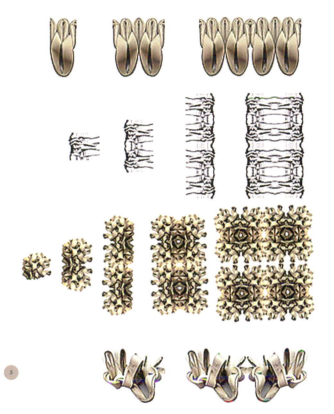

3 / 4 / 5
**Research from books,
magazines and fabric stores**
Jie collected research from books and
magazines in order to learn how to knit.

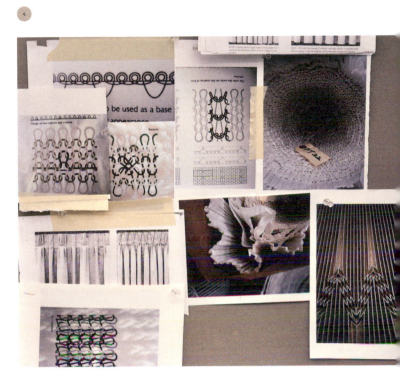

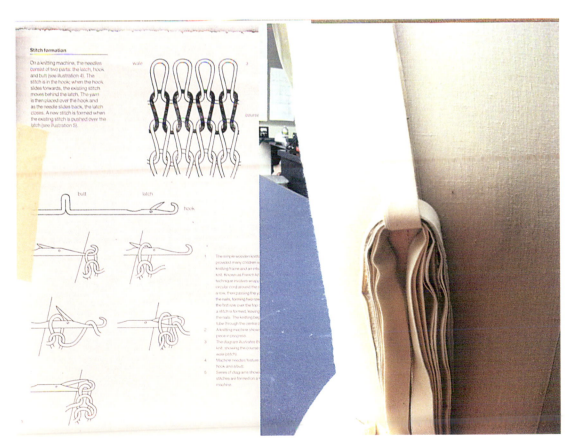

Idea to concept

During this phase, Jie began working with fabric to test out various techniques and investigate which materials worked best. She began by cutting six strips of calico (muslin) 3/4" x 1 yard (approx 2cm x 1m) and ironed each one to create pleats. (She calculated that she needed six strips to emulate the knit stitch in the diagram.)

This long pleated strip of calico was used as 'yarn', which Jie then used to 'knit', following the pattern of knit stitches. At first she pinned these strips in place on a flat table and changed the tension, making it tight or loose to see what would happen. Sometimes she could not follow the exact way of knitting due to the bulk of the pleated, woven fabric, so she was forced to find another solution and create a new fabric manipulation.

She also 'draped' or 'knitted' the strips on the dress form to explore the result, changing the size of the loops, the number of layers of strips in a loop and the ways of 'knitting'. Jie recognized the repetitive nature of the act of knitting and sought to replicate this with her fabric manipulation technique. She mirror-imaged the stitches in Photoshop to create new shapes and draped these on the dress form. Jie also documented her process with photography.

The first experiment done on the table resulted in a flat look that was reminiscent of fabric, but the second experiment on the dress form created a more 3D look and was more successful. It is important to try multiple approaches to your process in order to push ideas forward. Innovation often comes out of experimentation

6 / 7 / 8
Draping on the dress form
Jie experimented with layering different pleats and fabrics on the dress form.

and not knowing what comes next. While it is good to have a grasp of technique, in Jie's case her lack of knowledge about knitting inspired an entirely new approach and result.

Jie layered pleated fabric to create different shapes and also experimented with different types of pleats: accordion, pineapple, boxes, and mixed pleat (accordion and pineapple), finally deciding that the accordion pleat worked best. She also created her own technical drawing with instructions in order to help remember how to make the garment and how each technique was created.

In addition to the development of the 3D draping, Jie also incorporated crochet into her process and mixed this with her woven techniques; she combined woven pleating, knitting and rope crochet together to begin to create her approach to garment design.

As she worked on the dress form, Jie had no preconceived notion of how her technique would work; she was simply responsive to the movement of the fabric strips. Although she used the enlarged images of knit stitches as a starting point, she quickly moved into new territory as she discovered things that did and didn't work within the act of doing. This hands-on discovery led to new concepts and ideas that she would almost certainly not have developed on paper alone. This is important to note as students often assume that design can only happen in a 2D sphere. In fact, Jie had not done any initial design development in 2D other than the digital component that was used to manipulate her 3D work.

6

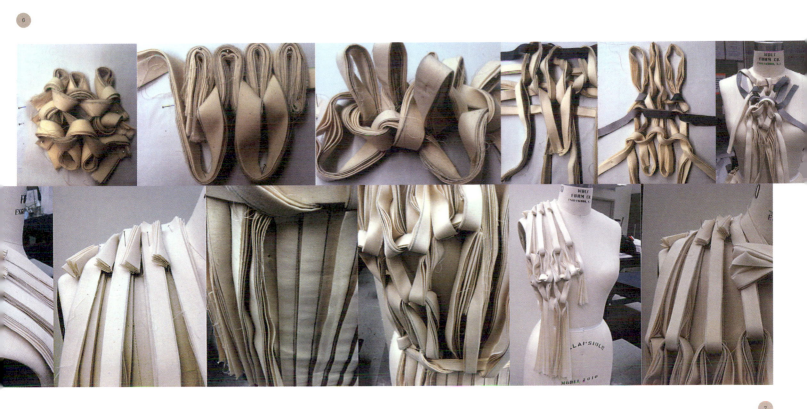

7

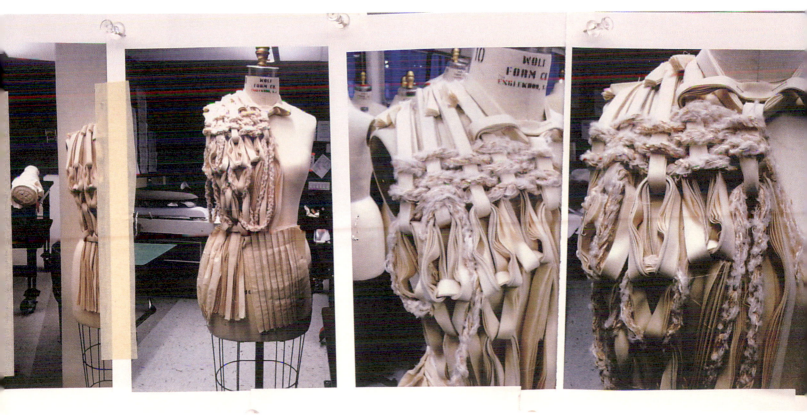

8

Turn to page 102 to see PART II (Concept) of this project, or page 166 for PART III (Design).

Functional separates, designed for longevity and adaptation.

Process

Video	Problem solving	Self-reflection
2D sketching	Technical flat sketching	Journaling
Brainstorming		Final editing
List making	Visual merchandising	2D styling
Journaling	Designing 'piece-by-piece'	Knitwear development
Textile development	Design editing and research	Flat sketching
Colour	Textile development	Fabrication
Silhouette	Journaling	2D final presentation
Customization	Narrative	

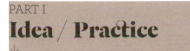

Growth and Decay
Andrea Tsao

This 2D project was undertaken in Andrea's third year of study at Parsons The New School for Design. It was a response to an in-class design brief with the end goal of designing a capsule collection of five to seven looks. The overarching premise was to investigate the intentionality of the process itself in the work of the artist and sculptor Andy Goldsworthy, and to look at his approach to the activity of creating art. Andrea then had to relate this to her own process as she 'built' a collection from her response to Andy's work. The key themes she considered were the juxtaposition of transience and permanence, brutality and beauty and growth and decay. The challenge became how to portray how these themes resonated within Andrea's own approach to design.

Often, designers utilize the work of an artist as a starting point or reference as they begin the process of designing a collection. This is not to say they will be directly imitating the work of the artist but merely that they will utilize this theme as a context within which to begin their process of research. In this case, Goldsworthy's work served as a backdrop to provide insight into a working methodology.

Andy Goldsworthy is a British sculptor, photographer and environmentalist living in Scotland, UK. He produces site-specific sculpture and land art situated in natural and urban settings. His art involves using natural and found objects to create both temporary and permanent sculptures, which draw out the character of their environment.

Andrea researched further into Goldsworthy's life as a sculptor, photographer and environmentalist. She felt that he came across much better in the documentary than on paper: 'It is seeing him work in nature, hearing the words he says, and the general mood and atmosphere surrounding his work that I find the most incredible. He loves being where he is, cherishes what nature has to offer him, and is stunned at nature's ability to give him materials to work with, only to suddenly take it away moments later. His work embraces time, permanence, delicacy, and balance. He builds beautiful structures from the shapes and colours he finds around him, often making natural sculptures that are in unexpected places and are expected to wash away with the rain, or be blown away by the wind. His attitude towards that thought is not resentful, but rather to marvel at that which grows and decays.'

Goldsworthy's approach to his work and the themes that arose are what fascinated Andrea most and became what she finds captivating.

Where did the idea come from?

Andrea's process takes a linear form, working consistently through her process from one stage to another, building a body of research that informs her approach to design.

The first step in the process was to watch the documentary *Rivers and Tides*, which looks at the daily activities of Goldsworthy as he goes about making art. Andrea then documented her own response as she watched the film, making notes, sketching, developing connections to her work from his. She collected images from particular projects that inspired her from Goldsworthy's work. These acted as a starting point and from here, she built her own ideas in the same manner Goldsworthy worked, incorporating the themes outlined in her journal.

Andrea found Goldsworthy's work extremely inspirational due to his own specific perspective on the process itself, along with the final outcome of his work. This made her question her own process and as a result she endeavoured to make new breakthroughs. Rather than being inspired by specific imagery, Andrea decided to embrace Goldsworthy's free-form, natural approach in an attempt to diversify from previous collections she had designed.

1 / 2
Work wear
As part of her enquiries into permanence and transience, Andrea looked at uniforms and work wear.

Goldsworthy's work embraces time, permanence, delicacy and balance. He builds beautiful structures from the shapes and colours he finds around him.... **Andrea Tsao**

3 / 4

Andy Goldsworthy

British artist Andy Goldsworthy was a big influence on Andrea's project. She found his approach to his work and the temporal nature of his sculptures captivating and inspiring.

Moving ideas forward

Building on the themes of permanence and transience, Andrea began to explore the ideas of permanence and impermanence in clothing. Apparel often loses a sense of permanence because of its temporal lifespan, driven by trends; heralded by the fashion elite for a season, only to be discarded the next. She found it interesting to imagine a time where trends are no longer important and where clothing only gets discarded when it no longer fits. As a solution, Andrea began to imagine designing clothes where the most likely places of wear and tear (armpits, waist, elbows and knees) are elastic and adjustable by drawstrings.

Durability has long been a focus of those who created work wear and uniforms. Andrea's idea was an extension of this, but it became more about the ability to change and alter the silhouette of one's garments from a personal customization standpoint. Traditionally, designers would have made use of techniques such as padding and topstitching to give durability and functionality to work wear. But where these would have created a tight rigidness to the clothes, Andrea was keen for her collection to feel loose and adaptable. Drawstrings were a simple, immediate solution; carefully placed, these would add flexibility to the design: functionally, in terms of fit, and aesthetically, in terms of the new scope for altering silhouette. Working out ideas in her sketchbook and writing out this concept allowed her to get inside the mind of the wearer and to execute the designs with a practical mindset.

In addition to the themes above, Andrea also wanted to explore Goldsworthy's method of being forced to respond to what already exists in nature. She translated this in the form of textile development and instead of using artificial chemical dyes, she opted for dyeing methods from a book called *Natural Dyeing* by Jackie Crook and experimented on broadcloth and various silks to see what types of textiles she could develop. Emulating Goldsworthy's pattern of responding to existing elements along with the theme of decay, she found rotting vegetables in her fridge that had naturally turned shades of green and brown and mixed them together in a pot of boiling water along with her fabric. She discovered that the only difference was that the colours came out less saturated and decided to use some of these home-made textiles in her designs.

5 / 6

Sketchbook development
Andrea's sketchbook kept track of her research, thought processes and ideas.

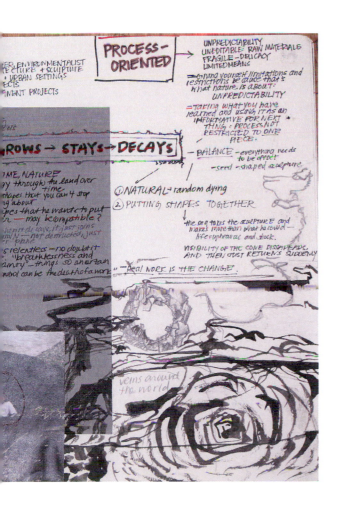

Idea to concept

In this next phase, Andrea wanted to interpret the ideas she had generated from Goldsworthy's process into a concept that she could call her own. Her goal was to make garments with natural shapes and organic silhouettes, responding to nature as he does in his work. The colours were dictated by nature's autumnal, earthy palette, so she wanted to play with boldness and shape experimentation, silhouette alteration and unconventional layering using delicate embellishments (much like Goldsworthy's work).

Out of her previous explorations, Andrea decided that the collection's conceptual core was the growth and decay of nature and how this theme could be achieved in clothing. Garments should have cut-outs with drawstrings in specific areas so that they can expand and shrink in accordance with the wearer's fluctuation in body size and shape. She explored the challenge of permanence within clothing, and played with silhouette personalization, as well as the reality of being able to adapt and tailor garments after purchase, to fit the various changes that occur within the body: 'We, as humans, are also beings of nature, and like the transience of the materials Goldsworthy saw around him, we cannot predict what will happen to our own body. We must adapt in the same way he was able to, and thus the drawstrings and ability to change the way your clothes fit you based on expansion and contraction over time is critical.'

Designers are problem solvers and the problem to be solved was how exactly Andrea would create a collection that embraced the whimsical yet serious mood of Andy's work and the shapes and colours of his sculptures, while establishing her own concept within her collection.

Her next phase of concept development would be driven by this challenge.

Turn to page 108 to see PART II (Concept) of this project, or page 172 for PART III (Design).

Graphic imagery translated into three-dimensional silhouettes via innovative knitwear techniques.

Process

2D/3D visualization	Idiom	2D / 3D editing
Photography	2D editing	3D sketching
3D reconstruction	3D draping	3D knit / textile innovation
3D draping	2D sketching	
3D shape / form	Textile / knit development	3D draping
	2D visualization	3D construction
	Photography	Colour / fabrication
	Digital technology	Technical knit development
	Knit innovation	Editorial photography

Trompe L'Oeil

Sara Bro-Jørgensen

This collection was Sara's final project for her Masters Degree at the Royal College of Art in London, UK. Her specialization in knitwear meant that her designs were very much about textures and pattern: 'I decided to do knitwear because I like the fact that I am in control of the whole design, meaning the development of both the fabric and shape.

Additionally, Sara's project was selected as one of the top ten collections to be presented at the prestigious ITS#NINE international festival in Trieste, Italy. ITS# stands for International Talent Support and is a platform for creative minds that has as a core goal 'to give visibility, support and a voice to young talent from every corner of the earth'. The collections are shown in front of an internationally acclaimed jury including: Viktor & Rolf, Sara Maino (Vogue Italia), Renzo Rosso (Diesel) and Nina Nitsche (Maison Martin Margiela).

I decided to do knitwear because I like the fact that I am in control of the whole design... **Sara Bro-Jørgensen**

Where did the idea come from?

The project began in a linear way. Sara had a specific idea to develop a collection from a series of photographs and in so doing to transform 2D images into 3D shapes. She began by taking a series of black and white photographs with an old plastic camera. The first day, she shot several rolls of film, intuitively seeking out everything she found interesting, including buildings, landscapes and people on the street.

She then selected the images she found most inspiring: a mix of graphic photos composed of lines, contrasting shapes and dreamy images with light coming through layers of thin fabrics. At this stage, Sara again edited the group, choosing only the best abstract images of building parts – composed of lines and layers of back-lit fabric – and discarded those of the people on the street.

For Sara, what began in a linear manner took on a random approach that was then harnessed back into a more specific direction. This process of reacting instinctively to the collected material is key to the design process, as one often stumbles across a new direction and this can bring new meaning and insight. These moments should not be ignored and each step should inform the next.

1

2

3

Experimenting with photography
Sara found that the images that inspired her most tended to be those that were composed of lines, contrasting shapes and light.

Moving ideas forward

With these images in mind, Sara shot more photos. This time she draped clothes and fabric on the body to recreate the dreamlike imagery she had captured in the first set of photos.

The clothes were a mix of existing garments from her wardrobe and garments from previous projects.

Sara deliberately chose garments with opposing qualities to create the sorts of contrasts reminiscent of the original photographic imagery. For example, a long, thick, black knitted scarf, a white tulle dress with many layers of fabric, and a jacket from a previous project in dark colours with all-over fringe. Here, Sara's method became more informed by the initial process itself as she sought to mirror the 2D process by making connections directly to silhouette. A second set of images was shot in a dark room, using only the light from a flash. This made the pictures look more abstract and almost transparent in places.

Again, Sara's intentionality drove the process forward. Everything she did was considered and instinctive: her selection of the images and garments, how she draped them to mimic the abstraction she captured in 2D within her 3D process… each step built on the one before and focused her ideas in a specific way.

Sara chose the strongest photographs as the basis for her project. Some would direct 3D shape while others would inform fabrication or surface print and pattern. It was quite easy to select the groups of images as some were clearly about layering fabric and others, like the ones where Sara was draping fabric on the body, were more focused on silhouette. These two directions dictated Sara's design choices: the layering of fabric and shape and silhouette created.

4 / 5 / 6
Draping on the body
Sara shot more photos, this time capturing clothes and shapes on her body to mimic the dreamlike quality of her earlier images. In some cases, she used double exposures to instil this quality further.

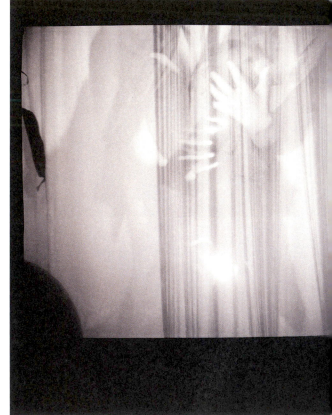

Idea to concept

For Sara the concept emerged organically. By selecting images and putting them into groups, the concept became clearer. She moved the project forward from 2D imagery to 3D design by focusing on each group individually. For example, she developed graphic prints from one selection of images, shapes from another group and in the end combined all the development into one design/garment.

Turn to page 114 to see PART II (Concept) of this project, or page 178 for PART III (Design).

Experiments in new technology and materials.

Process

Social media research	3D draping	3D drape
2D photography	Textile development	Editing
2D flat pattern	Wearable technology	Collaboration
Repurposing	Fabric innovation	Textile development
Collaboration	3D construction	3D construction / innovation
	3D experimentation	Self-reflection
		2D collage

PART I	PART II	PART III
Idea / Practice	Concept/Practice	*Design / Practice*
↓	~~120~~	~~184~~

Light Painting

Leah Mendelson

This project was part of Leah's Design Level 4 class, during her final year of study for her BA Fashion Design program at the Academy of Art in San Francisco. The original prompt for the project was part of the CFDA Geoffrey Beene scholarship submission, where the challenge was to design a collection in line with some part of Beene's aesthetic. Leah connected with his youthful, often whimsical approach to design and of course his emphasis on geometry (the famed, pattern-cut triangle).

Where did the idea come from?

Within the context of any design brief, Leah typically begins her design process with research: 'Research is very important for me, and I let myself go deep into issues that seem unrelated to fashion at all.' For this project, she started with her interests in science, time perception, esoteric symbolism, or anything else that she considered to fall under 'The Big Picture'. She started at the library, where she could readily access the Internet, physical books, magazine archives, and film. Focusing on the movement of energy within the body, Leah investigated a broad range of information including biology, acupuncture and esoterics.

Leah discovered a similar visual theme running through these completely different schools of thought; each had different scientific representations of the human figure, with lines running through them. Whether this took the form of lines of 'Chi' between meridian points, or the circulatory system, they all purported that there was an 'energy' or 'life force' running through our bodies at all times. She found that, at this early stage in the process, she occasionally felt less in control. It is important to highlight here the unpredictability of research in its truest form. Often, it is difficult to let go at this stage, as the focus on the end result stifles creativity and innovation: 'It can be tough starting off knowing that I'm interested in something for which there is no end, or single answer. But there are many answers, and I continue online or in books searching a stream of research that goes in unexpected places. I let go of thinking about the final project/ collection, and go along for the ride my curiosity takes me on.'

For Leah, it is clear that the excitement of knowing that she will end up somewhere beyond her current ideas is what makes the research process such a joy. It makes her feel that she is participating in something beyond her own preconceived notions of what is possible, practical, or what she 'should' be doing or who she should be. By letting go within the research process and following her thirst for knowledge, she develops a more open and spontaneous attitude.

1 / 2 / 3

Light painting

Light painting records the movement of a light source. It was the blurring of boundaries between still image and film that Leah found so compelling.

4

Moving ideas forward

Leah discovered the art of light painting while on Facebook, where she saw light painting photos posted on a friend's page. She contacted the photographer and started to research light painting as an art form.

Light painting is a simple photographic technique where you move a source of light in a darkened room, with the camera's shutter open for longer than usual. By doing so, it 'records' the movement of the light source. In Leah's case, she added a flash at some points to capture the model.

Light photography is a cross between the medium of film and photography, capturing time passing, as a still photograph. Leah is attracted to new mediums that blur the boundaries between the still image and film. Many of her projects start from research into an art form that she then incorporates into the context of fashion.

Leah found the amount of creativity and the possibilities explored within this medium breathtaking and she was excited to apply it to her own project. She believed light painting was the most appropriate method to illustrate energy moving through the body; using light, with its ever-changing and luminous qualities, was a perfect way to illustrate the qualities of energy itself.

4

Setting up the photo shoot
Leah and the photographer constructed a 3D cube out of PVC pipe and LEDs on a wire frame.

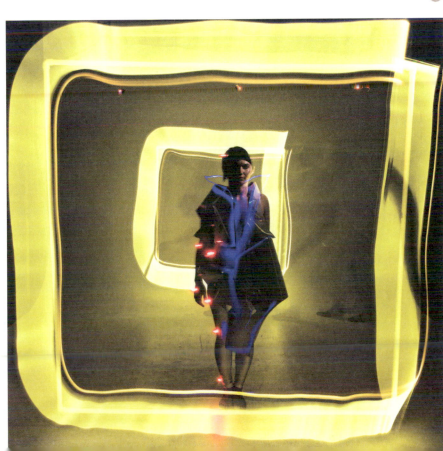

3

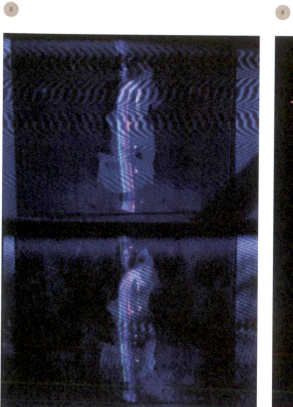

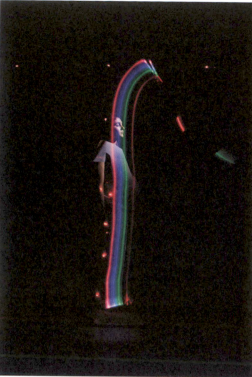

5 / 6 / 7 / 8 / 9
Draping with light
By capturing the movement of a light source, Leah was able to 'drape' light on the models.

Idea to concept

Leah decided to collaborate with the photographer, combining his technical knowledge with her design vision. They decided to build a 3D cube out of PVC pipe, with wires strung along it in the shape of a parabolic curve. They then hooked LEDs onto the wire, so that as they slid down the curve, they would capture it and create a light painting.

Leah was unclear how this related to her original idea for the photo shoot, but wanted to support the photographer's concept based on his expertise. She knew that to accomplish this complicated process and produce the results they hoped for would take many trials and more than one photo shoot. As she expected, during the shoot the concept didn't work. The LEDs moved down the wires at too slow a pace, and when the wire was angled more acutely to create more speed, the LED coin-battery configuration popped off and hit the ground. The visual results were more akin to light 'whimpers' than immaculate geometric beauty!

Leah used the photographer's light equipment along with some she found herself, because she wanted a variety of light objects to work with during the photo shoot. She used cathode lights (with a super-bright, electronic glow) along with electronic light sticks that changed colours and patterns. Leah used these light tools to 'drape' with – the trail of their glow captured to create shapes and silhouettes that would inform her process in design development.

In response to the light painting, Leah cut a pattern for a dress and stapled it onto the model. She had found the paper – a large, eight-foot advertising banner – on the street about a week prior. At the time she hadn't known what she would use it for, but her instincts told her to take it for future use.

The photographer brought in additional assistants for a second shoot, but there was some debate about the technical aspects of the project. Some felt that the amount of light Leah was recording would be overwhelming. But for her, experimentation was key, and she was convinced of her concept, so continued on. Sometimes, with collaborations, there are clashes of view and in this case it was a more prescribed, technical process versus Leah's risk-taking and proposition of a photographic style that seemed 'incorrect' in the eyes of the experts. The difference of opinions throughout proved challenging but Leah held her ground and moved beyond the formulaic approach to get the shots she wanted.

The final challenge was the release of the images. Since Leah had chosen to take an alternative route and shoot images that the photographer viewed as subpar, he was reluctant to release them to her. Leah viewed the project as a key experiment within her ideation process and every photo was a necessary documentation of that process, and vital to her project and the next stages of design development. In the end she was able to persuade him to give her the images she needed.

By working with a photography student, Leah had access to resources she didn't even know existed and this offered her options outside of the traditional realm of fashion. She didn't know exactly what the results of the photo shoot would be, and it was an exciting four hours.

9

Turn to page 120 to see PART II (Concept) of this project, or page 184 for PART III (Design).

Soft, draped silhouettes, suspended away from the physical body.

Process

Visual research	3D innovation	2D visualization
2D visualization	2D sketching	2D / 3D draping
3D concepts	3D draping	3D development
Observational research	Materiality	2D sketch line-up
Narrative research	3D construction	Editorial photography
3D construction	3D tailoring	

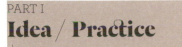

Tensegrity

Aura Taylor

The 'Tensegrity' project was one of five 2D portfolio projects Aura presented as part of her final review for her MFA in Fashion Design at the Academy of Art University in San Francisco. The project evolved from previous developments and research into biomimicry (the examination of nature's processes and systems and the application of these in order to solve human problems), and an investigation into acupuncture and the concept of tensegrity: a structural principle whereby individual elements are bound together by and within a structural system of continuous compression.

This project highlights the journey of design and the struggles therein. Designers move through a process of trial and error, and embracing the challenges is key to that journey. Here, Aura revisits a set of ideas from a prior project that she felt was unresolved. By moving her thought process forward in a new direction within a new sphere of research, she ended up developing a more complete concept.

My objective in this project was to maintain the organic quality of clothing, not just on the surface with conventional clothing shapes, but also from the perspective of construction. **Aura Taylor**

1

Olafur Eliasson

Inspired by the work of Danish-Icelandic artist Olafur Eliasson, Aura started out by imagining that she might translate her love of computer graphic geometry into a 3D design.

2 / 3 / 4

Visual research

As she added more and more layers, Aura was reminded of acupuncture. This led to further visual research in this area.

5

Imitating vector graphics with pins

Aura started out by experimenting with pins and thread on a dress form.

Where did the idea come from?

The initial idea for this project had a random beginning and came about spontaneously. While looking through her personal inspiration image library, Aura was naturally drawn to a number of vector graphics that she had collected over time and started to wonder how she might translate these fine 2D vector lines into precise 3D geometric patterns.

Aura started out by experimenting with pins and thread on a dress form. On the back of the dress, she created a circle with the pins and started mapping the thread from one to another, going back and forth between certain points, imitating the computer-generated vector graphics.

As Aura added more and more layers of thread and extended a new pattern towards the front, she was reminded of acupuncture, and so began researching its practice and philosophy further.

She rearranged the pins on the dress form according to each acupuncture point, and by connecting these points with a string of thread, created a 3D lace that now symbolized the channels of bioenergy flow.

As Aura researched the idea, it expanded further and moved away from simply imitating the 2D computer graphics in 3D lines to a whole concept of mapping the invisible or 'hidden world' of live energy. The subject of energetic channels and blueprints of acupuncture points captivated her, but she was also thinking of the bigger picture to gain an overall sense of where this philosophy would fit in and how it was relevant for today.

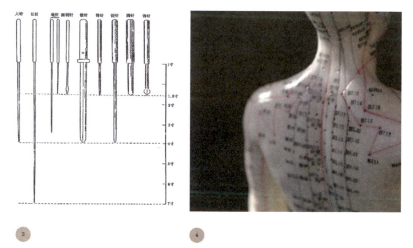

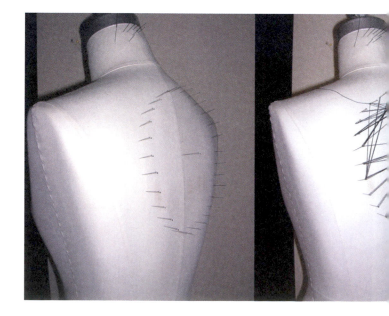

As an observer of social climate and guided by her own intuition and points of view, in further readings Aura came across the ideas of biomimicry, well-being, and healing. Biomimicry, or 'nature as a model' is a science that studies patterns, systems and structures occurring in nature and then imitates or takes inspiration from these models to create solutions in design that improve products. Biomimicry also tells us that every solution we seek has already been designed by nature, thus if we find ways to reconnect with it, we will find well-being. In this instance, Aura used acupuncture as the inspirational model of balancing vital energy in nature.

'We are living in accelerated times. Everyone and everything seems to be moving rapidly. The frequency with which information bombards us is staggering. People constantly talk about feeling over-amped and overwhelmed. I believe that this is a perfect time to consider "energetic rebirth." There are myriad of ways in which we become depleted; working beyond what our body tells us is supportive, feeling energetically low because we eat the wrong foods, don't exercise, or give power to people that drain us of the vital life force we need for wellness. All these things can be handled if we become more conscious. We have to become aware of how we use and transmit energy in order to create life-enhancing energy within and around us. With this collection I aim to raise awareness and inspire change in the area of well-being.'

As Aura continued her research and looked for more visual references to expand her theory, she came across an article in *Viewpoint Magazine* on future communities.

The article proposed that by 2050, 80 per cent of the earth's population would be residing in an urban centre and that this would increase the gap between humans and nature. It suggested that this would trigger a rise of new communities referred to as 'Rurbans' and 'Healthburbans'. The latter would be preoccupied by living healthy lifestyles, finding wisdom in ancient philosophies and practising in meditation, exercise and healthy diet. This new generation would live in urban-metro areas of the world and enjoy all the benefits of modern living, yet would be constantly searching for a reconnection with their energetic source through body and mind.

Aura was impacted by the ideas presented in the article and this encouraged her to move her concept forward. She sought ways to express its philosophy in material form. She was reassured that her idea as an overall concept was important within the context of the future of design, not just personally but globally: 'This "Healthburban" image not only communicated a sense of calmness and ancient wisdom to me, but the visual reference compelled me to consider exploring Grecian draping and non-Western clothing. In the beginning I dismissed the idea of draped dress, simply because it was not the way I envisioned the look of the collection (that would bridge the gap between metropolitan living and the laws of nature) nor would it satisfy my personal aesthetic. However, later in the process after dropping the threading idea, I returned to it as the main visual for the mood of the Tensegrity collection, because I felt it was appropriate for the concept. Later, I introduced more controlled draping through geometry with the help of the metal strut construction, in order to balance the feel of modern with something calm and familiar as draping.'

This reinforces the importance of continuing research in search of support of a theory you may have. Aura had been searching for ways to contextualize her concept, not only within her own design process, but also within the larger, global picture. Her findings confirmed her initial instincts and led her forward in this direction, bringing together these two desires.

5

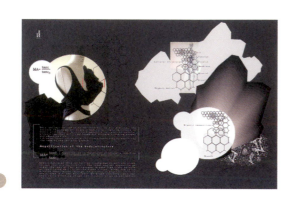

6 / 7 / 8
Mapping the invisible
As she worked, Aura found links
between the patterns of biological
bodies and the patterns of natural
structures such as stars and galaxies.
But after unsuccessful results in
design developments following this
route, she decided to change course
slightly.

Idea to concept

Zooming in and out of the body through her researched
visuals, Aura was able to see how different geometric
patterns of biological bodies (acupuncture points on
the human body, stars and galaxies, structures in
plants, cells, soundwaves, etc.), repeat themselves in
different scales and objects.

Oneness stood out as a conclusion to all of Aura's
observations. Starting with one pin representing the
acupuncture point, she had discovered how everything
in nature and the universe is connected and how this
invisible world of nature's vital forces acts based on the
laws of the universe without any effort: 'Biology and
fashion seem like a contradiction in terms – biology
standing for everything that is alive, vital and organic,
and fashion for the superficial and man-made. Is it
possible to reconcile the two? In an earlier collection
"Hidden World", I had attempted to unite these two
seeming polarities. I looked for answers by travelling
in and out of the physical human body and translating
studies of biological phenomenon into clothing.'

'"Hidden World" was a wearable art collection based
on biomimicry, consisting of two capsule groups.
Both drew inspiration directly from the human body,
challenging design methods, and taking the idea of
fashion beyond material goods. As I seek aesthetic
expression in fashion, I try to break out of controlled,
standardized methods, and repetitive patterns and
processes of clothing design. My objective in this
project was to maintain the organic quality of clothing,
not just on the surface with conventional clothing
shapes, but also from the perspective of construction.'

Having carried out this initial investigation into
bioenergy in the human body, Aura carefully analysed
and organized nature's phenomenon into geometric
shapes and structures. These structures eventually
became rational representations of anatomical forces in
clothing design.

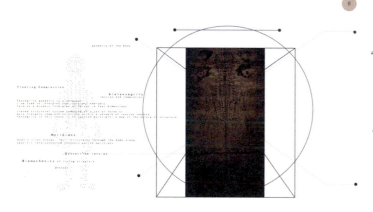

7

8

Moving ideas forward

The next step, which is typical in Aura's process,
was to connect her idea to the concept by creating a
vocabulary. At this stage she wrote out key words from
her research and checked definitions and relationships
to other words in the dictionary. As a result, key words
emerged such as wholeness, healing and meditation.
For example, 'a centred mind' denoted a state of focus
that incorporates a total togetherness of body and mind,
calm, stillness and oneness: 'I treat this phase as a
journey of discovery of learning, expecting to arrive at
new insights that will further direct my design process
and/or visual expression. Usually, after this phase I'm
able to clearly define the concept and know exactly
which elements will become a visual representation or
the language of my philosophy.'

After unsuccessful results in design development and in the search for a new solution, Aura came across the concept of tensegrity, or 'floating compression'.

'Tensegrity is a structural principle based on the use of isolated components in compression inside a net of continuous tension, in such a way that the compressed members (usually bars or struts) do not touch each other and the prestressed tensioned members (usually cables or tendons) delineate the system spatially.' [1]

Seeking further ideas and engineering solutions for the 3D construction of garments, Aura explored the work of noted engineer, Buckminster Fuller, a pioneer in global thinking and the first to coin the term 'tensegrity.' She also returned to her process of word mapping to create a new vocabulary and further expand the concept, this time taking a different direction based on her new research and inspiration. Key words included: material efficiency, architecture, energy, synergy, tensegrity, tension, and biotensegrity (the muscular-skeletal system as a synergy of muscle and bone).

After researching tensegrity and its analogy to biological forces – its reinterpretation through an abstract and strictly geometric, structural principle – Aura felt this was an appropriate aesthetic and construction solution to restart the project. This was the connection that she had been searching for, the link between biology and fashion, between the seeming polarities of everything that is alive, vital and organic, and the superficial and man-made. She decided to use the principles of tensegrity within the garments and once again chose to interpret and represent the central theme of anatomic geometry and the interplay of forces within living bodies.

Her concept had become solidified through a process of trial and error, and a journey through various challenges. She was now committed to building garments on the tensegrity principle, with a simple exposed strut construction that would hold the garment's shape while allowing it to extend away from the body.

1. Gomez-Jauregui (2010) *Tensegrity Structures and their Application to Architecture.*

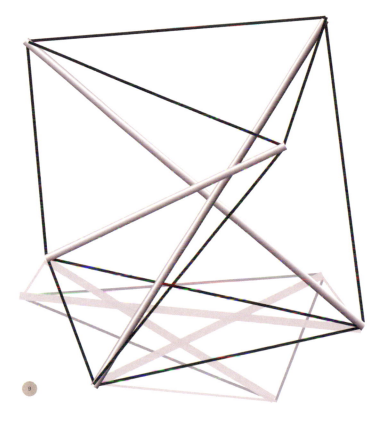

9

Tensegrity

It was at this point that Aura came across the idea of 'tensegrity'. Tensegrity is a structural principle whereby individual elements are bound together by and within a structural system of continued compression.

Turn to page 126 to see PART II (Concept) of this project, or page 190 for PART III (Design).

An investigation into shape-memory materials and new craft technologies and textiles.

Process

Investigation of craft

Data collection

Material / scientific research

Journaling

Material / scientific experimentation

Visual research

2D sketching

Fusion weaving

Fibre experimentation

Craft

Tradition and technology

Embroidery

Weaving

Natural / artificial technology

Organic engineering

Natural programming

Techno Naturology

Elaine Ng Yan Ling

Elaine Ng Yan Ling earned her MA in Design for Textile Futures (graduating with distinction) at Central Saint Martins College of Art and Design in London, UK, exploring the function of shape-memory materials. She focused on how the behaviour of natural elements can be manifested in man-made materials to enhance modern architecture and interior design. 'Techno Naturology' was Elaine's MA thesis project.

Elaine's design principle is based on biomimicry, focusing on a hybrid materialization of craft and technology. By programming shape-memory materials, she explored how movement can be achieved through natural responses to heat, light and electricity, and how woven and etched patterns respond to changes in environmental conditions such as light, intensity or mechanical force. With a sustainable and eco-conscious design philosophy, Elaine explores living urban textiles and their responses to sun, wind and rain.

Techno naturology (the use of artificial technology to activate and simulate natural reactions) is Elaine's latest discovery in the relationship between natural formations and technology design. Her collection received the New Design Britain Award 2011 for Surfaces at Interiors, Birmingham, UK. She recently received a TED fellowship.

Where did the idea come from?

This project concentrates on understanding how the property of materials can become a craft technique. Elaine's initial idea began with the pure fascination of shape-memory material and how its physical property impacts its relevance within the design industry. The project aims to explore the function of and symbiotic relationship between shape-memory alloy/polymers and the natural sensing system of wood. The intrinsic qualities of natural and artificial materials are investigated using the hybrid tectonic system to challenge preconceived limitations and increase the potential of textiles. The first stage of developing her idea focuses on understanding the physical property of the materials themselves.

Traditional design methodology includes primary research and secondary data collection. In this case, Elaine's initial research is divided into two parts: Part One – Science-inspired data collection and Part Two – Investigating how traditional weaving with natural materials, such as cane (which is less controllable) and programmable microcontrollers can coexist.

The choice of research methods initially grew out of Elaine's personal interest in physics and the methodology used within laboratory experiments; finding results through revelation. Traditionally, scientists often conclude that negative data collection is not useful and a waste of time. However, as a textile designer, Elaine finds this process very interesting. She has taken the traditional, logical data collection within science and applied this approach within design.

Elaine's next step in her research was to explore nature's ability to constantly evolve. She chose to research the flexibility of wood veneer since the properties of wood are very close to the properties of the shape-memory material she planned to use. Since this is a material-led project, wood veneer is a good choice because of its natural shape-memory ability. The warpage within the wood that most people see as a disadvantage Elaine views as a distinct plus as it provides a good contrast between artificial and natural shape-memory materials.

Elaine visited different veneer manufacturers and talked to furniture and wood experts in order to understand the natural behaviour and different varieties of wood grain available. She collected different types of veneer with various grains, including birds-eye maple, walnut and teak, while at the same time reading about the biology of veneer. This approach reflects first-hand primary research, where information is gathered to support the potential development of an idea into a concept.

On a micro level, Elaine learnt that wood grain continuously grows in the direction of sunlight and that humidity can affect its appearance. On a macro level, she discovered that the mechanical structure of a pine cone is influenced by its bilayer system. She also investigated the physical properties of smart materials such as shape-memory fibres, polymers and alloys and explored how external factors can influence their behaviour and appearances. For example, when you pass a current through a shape-memory alloy (such as nickel titanium), the alloy reacts and changes shape accordingly before returning to its original shape. Similarly, shape-memory polymers are affected through changes in temperature and can be moulded or stretched into any desired shape.

Elaine had to do extensive research in order to understand the properties and physics of the shape-memory material and arrangement of the particles. She had to learn how to read the physics graphs in order to understand the different types of alloys that exist and she called upon various shape-memory material suppliers and universities to get in touch with shape-memory mechanics who could explain the process further. This represents her intense commitment to the initial process of research and investigation.

If you don't have the information readily available, it is key to pursue experts who can provide further clarity. In this case, given the scientific context, Elaine needed to do extensive research beyond her field of knowledge in order to make the connections from science to textiles so important to her project.

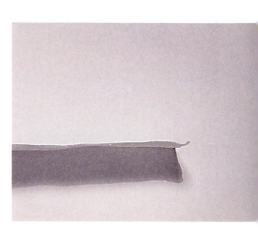

1

Material research

Shape memory alloys change shape and react to external stimulation such as heat.

2

A study of natural material mechanisms

Elaine studies pine cones and noted how they flexed in reaction to changes in humidity.

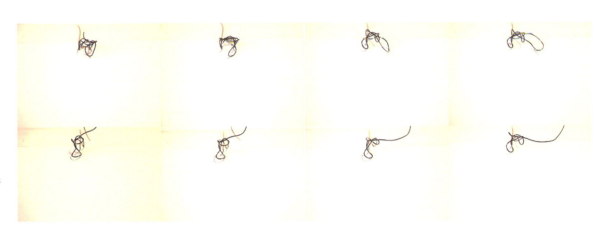

3

Materials testing

Elaine found that some shape memory alloys are already pre-programmed while others can be trained into desired shapes.

4

Shape memory polymers

Soft polymers soften and become malleable when they are in contact with hot air or hot water.

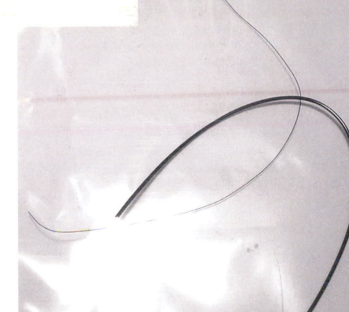

Moving ideas forward

Elaine moved her ideas forward in two distinct directions: primary scientific research, and design research. She demonstrated intense depth in her approach by investigating themes in several ways, including data collection, material and scientific research and surveys.

Using the research she had collected, Elaine kept a diary documenting the behaviour of the raw samples and noted how the external stimuli (temperature, moisture, electrical current and sunlight) changed their appearance.

In order to develop her ideas further, Elaine had to experiment with the physical samples of both the natural wood-based shape-memory materials, and the artificial shape-memory alloys, polymers and fibres. She did this by testing their differing behaviour and reactions to water and moisture, current and voltage respectively. Elaine documented her experimentation in two ways: by keeping a natural and an artificial logbook. Within the natural logbook, she began testing ideas that could affect natural behaviour; for example, how moisture can be introduced when designing wood, and how the 'weathering' process could also be part of the design process. She prioritized the test of the weathering process, since the result would take the longest.

Within the artificial logbook, Elaine recorded information such as the currents tested, the types of sensors used and the behaviour of the alloy, on video. She discovered that when the electrical current passed through the alloy, it gave out heat and often the heat caused damage to the textiles. All these experiments allowed her to gain understanding of the properties of the shape-memory alloy. In order to find out how to write a good code to program and control the circuit and to understand which sensor was best to use to communicate between the space and the user, Elaine tested the circuit with LED light. This was the most efficient and visible way to communicate whether the circuit was responding or not.

Parallel to the science-inspired data collection, Elaine also developed surveys and questionnaires for the general public. She wanted to discover if they perceived where and how movement could be generated in material within space and if they understood how structures or surfaces related to tectonic movement. Within this exercise, Elaine asked the respondents to create folding structures out of paper. This exercise tested the concept of developing tectonic movement surfaces and also enabled Elaine to avoid creating a completely alien concept that was difficult to understand.

For her design inspiration Elaine made connections between the qualities of the shape-memory materials and the growth of cortical bone within the brain because their physical properties share the common properties of elasticity and plasticity. She collected medical scans and researched the movement of the cortical folding within the brain and compared its physical appearance to the growth of tree roots (highlighting the parallels of growing within a confined space and thus moulding their shape to their surroundings.

The sketchbook research at this stage included collecting physical samples of wood veneer and creating imprints of tree bark and roots. This process allowed Elaine to understand how these organic shapes were formed. Taking the imprints (or rubbings) allowed her to understand how the weathering process can produce a three-dimensional texture. This variety of first-hand research inspired Elaine's drawings and sketching in this first stage and directly influenced the appearance of the later stages of her work.

5 / 6

Primary research
Elaine collected first-hand data to investigate things such as how weathering can become part of a design process, and how folding fabric can create organic forms.

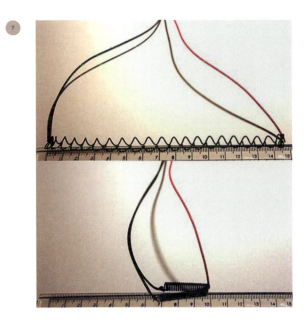

7

Collecting data

Here, Elaine was testing the speed of reaction in a shape memory allot when an electrical current is passed through it.

8

Diagrammatic representation

Here, Elaine creates a schematic diagram of the reactions in the pine cone.

Idea to concept

After collecting all the information about the shape-memory materials, Elaine had a better understanding of how each material could be manoeuvred through the effects of external stimuli: heat, water and current. The idea of extracting the responsive behaviour from nature and mimicking it through design is a fundamental component of a design principle called biomimicry (mimicking the behaviour and engineering of nature). The natural responsive system is nature's way of responding to its surroundings. Biomimicry has become a very influential phenomenon, particularly in recent years within the field of functional design.

After experimenting with various types of shape-memory material, Elaine better understood the similarities between artificial shape-memory materials and natural wood substances. In the next phase in the design process she experimented with paper forms similar to pop-up book structures, created by sewing paper and wooden materials together. Within this stage Elaine identified some problems: she would always have to initiate a movement before the structure 'popped up' and the interactivity was very stiff. The movement was repeatedly the same and boring to look at. Hence this inspired her to investigate a 'soft interaction', which involved more interaction with the surroundings: movement that was parallel to real time change and most importantly movement that was related to itself. As a result, Elaine came up with the concept of creating a hybrid material, concentrating on its behaviour and how its substance could change its appearance.

Elaine's concept was established out of these series of investigations. Her goal was to combine the understanding of the natural response system's behaviour with smart materials in order to create seamless tectonic movement, creating a controlled behaviour but with movement that is still influenced and dominated by the responsiveness of nature.

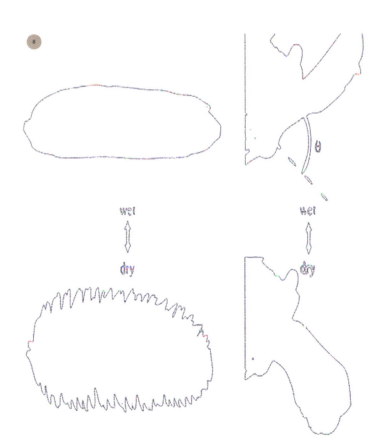

Turn to page 132 to see PART II (Concept) of this project, or page 196 for PART III (Design).

Academic Perspective
Jonathan Kyle Farmer

What is your design philosophy and how does this impact your teaching?

My design philosophy is simple: it's about discovering and defining self. I believe that as designers we are capable of changing the world: inventing, redefining, problem solving and not living by someone else's rules.

As I experience life I tune into as many channels as possible. I hear but, more importantly, listen to what it is the universe is telling me, enabling processes to grow through involved practices and dedication to subject. I apply this to my own work, considering that I am constantly renewing myself by reflecting and reinventing my own methodologies and systems.

This impacts my teaching daily; I encourage my students to approach design this way and to not get caught up in what they believe the industry is looking for. I strongly believe that we can each redefine what is meant by 'industry standards' by implementing our own systems, and providing evidence of both successful and non-successful practice by simply doing what is innate.

What methods do you use as an instructor to inspire students to excel beyond their limitations?

There are a number of fundamentals, two of which are: 'Total honesty' and 'Making it personal'.

'Total honesty' is not a method but more of a personal directive. There are always cultural and generational dyslexias but personal experience and a wide knowledge base inform the analysis. Speaking from an honest place and not sugar-coating feedback is vital to a student's growth.

'Making it personal' as a method highlights the importance of considering one's own personal aesthetic. But more importantly, to always contextualize, individualize and take into consideration that students come from a diverse range of backgrounds, circumstance and belief systems.

Can you describe any specific methodologies or frameworks you have developed in your teaching (that are unique to your approach)?

At the beginning of each project, I creatively brief my students. This would take into consideration my design paradigms and values, even within the design of the printed brief. Consideration of some theoretical basis, such as the understanding of visual literacy, also helps me to focus on every detail of the educational process: a key at this point is to take into consideration all communication details (verbal and non-verbal) within the class development.

I have been implementing a system that I have developed and built over the past seven years, based on the idea of 'cross-pollination' and the understanding of alternative design processes.

Also, the notion of play is natural within the design/ learning process. Play builds upon students' previous knowledge bases and gives them the opportunity to develop skills within their own frame of reference, while embedding every step of their new experiences alongside it.

I encourage students to be active participants in these processes but more importantly, to have fun and enjoy what they are doing by being aware of the different elements that occur during 'play'.

What is the source of your approach? How did it evolve?

As a person with dyslexia I think that my educational processes and strategies started to develop when I recognized that my learning experiences and ways of development were not always taken into consideration. This forced me to create my own language and as a result, drawing and visual language became my mother tongue. It helped me realize at a very early stage, the significance of recognizing that visual literacy skills within design education are equal to verbal literacy skills within other academic studies.

Jonathan Kyle Farmer, Associate Professor of Fashion Design at Parsons The New School for Design, NYC, graduated from the Royal College of Art, London, in 2000. Kyle has worked worldwide as a fashion designer and illustrator, and has taught at BFA and MFA level internationally. As a futurist, Kyle's approach as an educator and as a practising designer is one of exploration and innovation, challenging the general perception of what it is to be fashion designer.

Ultimately, I have found that the things I found most difficult to learn in childhood have become some of my strongest teaching tools: language, phonetics, semantics and word play. I ask students, 'What is a skirt? A dress? A coat?' and ask them to translate the words into various languages and back into English, then ask, 'What does it look like now?', 'What does it sound like?', 'And does it still function as the name it was originally given?'

When a student hits a wall in their process, how do you help them to move forward?

I believe that as an educator, my role is to help students understand that the 'hitting the wall' metaphor is actually not an obstacle, but instead 'the design process' itself. I encourage students to avoid predicting what the item might be, but instead to be open to the idea of allowing the design to become what it wants to become.

Do you think there is a 'right' or 'wrong' way to design?

I do not think there is a right way of designing. As mentioned before, we all are capable of finding and building our own design language.

Similarly, I would argue that every teacher has a different way of teaching. I do, however, think that there is a wrong way to teach, and this corresponds to the ways in which the teacher's 'design approach' or 'aesthetics' become imposed on the student, making decision-making a 'right or wrong' answer from the teacher's perspective.

Can you share your thoughts on the importance of the following:

Research: The foundations of any pyramid/project – if your research isn't solid then your foundation will fail, your process will not be strong. Research is more than data collecting; it is also discovered in the doing.

Experimentation/design development: Experimentation is what I consider 'play', and the design development the process of problem solving. Both are connected in this complementary and dynamic structure.

Process: Is simply the doing of something.

Vision/aesthetics/taste: I personally disagree with the idea of 'taste' and how it is related to aesthetic. Coming from personal values and individuality, I disagree with categorizing something as 'aesthetically correct'. There will always be those who do like your work and those who don't. The key is to define yourself and the rest comes along on the journey.

Identity as designer: It's all about your own identity, you find your own identity and people will recognize it and you in it. Never design with a customer in mind, if your identity is defined and your product is relevant your customer will find you. The idea of a muse, however, is a different story.

Self-reflection: Is the key to 'help you keep going', to understand your own processes, perceive the obstacles and be empowered by them.

If you could distil your approach in one sentence, what would that be?

Inspired individuality leads to innovation and invention.

What advice would you give to students or emerging designers who are still seeking to establish their identity and aesthetic?

Give your work context, understand how things have been done historically then stand up and say, 'this is now how I do it'. You can change the world, just by asking 'why?'

Designer Perspective
Siki Im

What is your design philosophy?

To create and propose a different perspective and viewpoint.

How do you work? What is the first step in your design process? Is it always the same?

It differs and I enjoy it that way. Sometimes because of timing, fabric selection comes first. Sometimes my sketchbook has priority, but it always starts with a feeling. It can be driven from the *New York Times*, a book, a movie, politics, social commentary, or a strong memory. I sketch a lot, make detail studies and mock-ups, experiment, and drape, before I finalize a design.

How did your design process evolve? Has the process changed over time?

The process is the same. I apply the same process when designing a space, graphics or music. The only variable that has changed is quantity.

Is your process instinctive or learned, or a combination of both?

It is very much both. I assume, as a trained architect, I tend to stick more with the intellectual part but I have been learning that fashion is very much an emotional process also, which is imperative.

But this is probably just due to time. It often takes years to design and build a building whereas in fashion you have to complete at least two collections per year, and often more. This inevitably means your design process is different and much faster. Through this speed you have to make quick decisions and have to design with your gut, which I think is good and more fun.

Do you understand your process to be linear (building one design from another) or somewhat random?

Sometimes I wish it would be more linear and therefore maybe easier. But then you don't give space for these beautiful 'happy accidents', where chance and improbability has no voice, and grace becomes stagnant.

This book addresses multiple entry points to design (first steps/inspiration): literal, narrative, abstract, 2D visual, 2D flat pattern, 3D deconstruction, 3D construction, narrative, mind mapping, textile innovation or new technologies. Which of these best describes your process?

I use all the methods mentioned above.

In my opinion, these various methods allow you to explore a deeper thought process and concept and check if it works or not. Personally, I get inspired by the *New York Times* – by the articles, current affairs, and very often the images themselves. I tend to use more social and critical issues for my inspiration. I really don't know why – maybe this is a way for me to compensate and make the concept 'deeper'? I do tons of sketches and make 3D mock-ups, fabric treatments, 3D computer programs, muslins and draping. Sometimes I use the computer to explore a certain design through diagrams; sometimes I do this with a traditional pen.

Born in Cologne, Germany, **Siki Im** moved to the UK and studied architecture at the Oxford School of Architecture. After working as an architect in various cities around the world, he started his career in fashion in New York City and was Senior Designer for both Karl Lagerfeld and Helmut Lang. In September 2009, Siki Im introduced his first solo collection in New York City, which won him the prestigious Ecco Domani award for Best Menswear in 2010 and in 2011 Im was awarded the Samsung Design & Fashion Fund. His collection is sold worldwide. He is currently adjunct faculty at Parsons The New School For Design, teaching senior concept design.

If you were to distil your approach to design in one sentence, what would that be?

Sometimes it is important to do something you hate.

When or if you hit a wall in your process, how do you move forward?

It is important to not get obsessed; you have to slow down, sit back, relax, and then have a look again. It is not easy to let go but it might put things in perspective. Or sometimes you need to walk away and things will unfold by themselves. It is also important that you talk and bounce ideas with your peers and your team.

Do you think there is a 'right' or 'wrong' way to design?

There is no real right or wrong, but as designer (in contrast to an artist or these days maybe not) you have to run a business with sale goals you need to achieve, so you can design the next season. Hence if a design does not sell it does not mean it is wrong or wrongly designed but maybe not applicable or just not 'good'.

Can you share your thoughts on the following in relation to your own process:

Research: Very, very important. This is the time where you can study, learn and explore.

Experimentation/design development: To create 'new' things – this is a very vital part of the process but it is also a luxury: time and money.

Process: I assume the more collections you do the more you find your own process. But, as mentioned above you need to keep it fresh and open for these beautiful accidents.

Vision/aesthetics/taste: It is always easiest when it is close to you and it is honest. You have to believe in it – it comes naturally.

Identity as designer: The identity is maybe the most important aspect; it gives stability and security as a designer and person, expresses an attitude as a brand, and it helps the consumer.

Self-reflection: As a human being this is essential; to be more aware and conscious of what is going on inside you and also what is going on around you – which means you are contemporary and aware. I believe this is necessary to create. These days where the market asks for more collections and faster floor changes, and the speed of media is overwhelming, it is hard to reflect and ponder.

What advice would you give to students or emerging designers who are still seeking to establish their identity and aesthetic?

To be honest and aware – this is maybe the easiest in the long run. If you are trying too hard it is more exhausting and people will know. Also, be open to changes and have fun.

Point of View

Talent Scout, Barbara Franchin
Director of ITS

Barbara Franchin is the Director and Project Supervisor of ITS (International Talent Support) and Head of the agency EVE, based in Trieste, Italy. She has also been responsible for the organization of this annual event since its inception in 2000. ITS is a talent scouting event to promote youth creativity in the realm of fashion, accessories and photography and is held in its native Trieste every July.

Among the most enthusiastic supporters of ITS is Diesel founder Renzo Russo and the juries of the competition have included designers such as Raf Simons, Hilary Alexander, Cathy Horyn and Viktor & Rolf.

She is recognized as one of the most important talent scouts of young fashion designers, accessories designers and photographers and was recently included by Italian *Elle* magazine as one of the 100 most powerful women in fashion.

What do you look for when viewing a new collection to include in ITS?

Basically, I'm looking for the creative spark. Apart from a designer with very strong technical abilities, I am looking for the unseen, for something that strikes me as different, as uncommon. I'm looking for a different order of things, something that has not been tried yet... As time goes by, it seems to get harder and harder.

What elements do you see as key in the development of a young designer? How do you assess raw talent?

It is very important – perhaps the most important thing – for a young designer to gain experience, to work for a brand or a company and learn all there is to know about the market and about the difficulties in surviving in today's market. I hear way too often about young designers wanting to launch their own brand immediately after finishing their studies. I can understand it, but in most cases it's the worst choice: there are way too many brands out there and surviving alone is terribly tough. I've seen a lot of young designers relying on wicked financers who allow them to access the money necessary to launch their brand, just to steal their creativity and leave them with nothing...

As for how you assess raw talent, well that's a tough one...It took me years of portfolio viewing and meetings with students to grow a sort of 'instinct' towards identifying raw talent. To me, it's mostly connected to the ability in finding the key to turn one's dream into something real, tangible. That's where talent steps in.

What do you look for in a strong portfolio? Are you looking for breadth and depth in the designer, an ability to deliver more than one standout collection?

Absolutely, yes. Being able to deliver one collection is just the starting point.

How do you assess this?

When you see a designer that is capable of translating in many different ways a single idea, to me that's when I see breadth and depth.

Do you want to see process in this component?

I want to understand how a designer went from A to B so yes, I need to understand the process; the journey that took him/her there.

Do you view the designer's process and approach to design as key in developing their vision, aesthetic and point of view as a designer? If so, please elaborate.

Certainly! I would say it all comes from there actually. I believe that a designer's point of view and aesthetics is shaped by how he/she approaches design. At least the designers I am interested in. Otherwise, it's just a production of items for the market to sell. There is no depth in producing something that doesn't have a reason, that doesn't come from a strong opinion on what the result should be, that isn't rooted in a profound research, in one's own ideas on their culture and surroundings. A design should be justified, and the perfect design should have its justification clearly and easily accessible for everyone to see and understand.

What makes a design 'good' or a collection successful?

I consider a design successful when I see a strong personalization, when a garment becomes a signature piece that immediately identifies the designer who made it. It can be a jacket, a pair of jeans, a shirt...it can be anything as long as it is immediately clear that there's something different, and that the difference is due to the maker.

Which is more important, commercial viability or creativity/vision? Or is a marriage of both desirable?

I'd say that the peak is when creativity and commercial viability go together. I do not like creativity per se. Pure and wild creativity is certainly beautiful, but in my opinion the biggest result for a designer is to turn their own creativity into something that can be bought and worn by everybody.

Who, in your opinion, do you view as the most successful emerging young designers and what sets them apart?

Aitor Throup is quite revolutionary in my opinion in the way he conceives fashion as purpose-driven. In him I see the perfect expression of a design that is justified. I see something that has never been tried before in his work. Mark Fast because nobody has ever produced knitwear the way he does. Michael Van der Ham for his ability to turn what looks like an apparent clash into a perfectly balanced outfit. Footwear designer Chau Har Lee, for her ability to produce shoes nobody had ever seen before. Heikki Salonen for the image of women he was able to portray... These are just the first that come to my mind.

What advice would you give to a fashion design graduate entering today's global marketplace?

Do not launch your own brand! Look for paid internships or job opportunities! Strengthen your abilities and learn from the market before daring to do your own things!

FASH
THI
PART II

cone

'Awareness of universals is called conceiving, and a universal of which we are aware is called a concept.'
Bertrand Russell

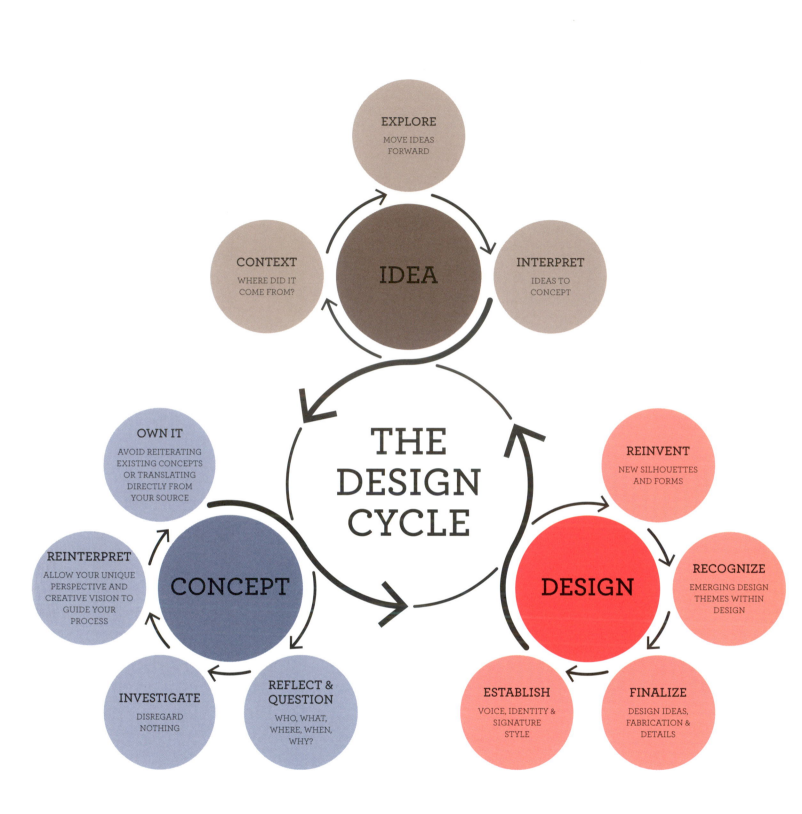

EXPLORE
MOVE IDEAS FORWARD

CONTEXT
WHERE DID IT COME FROM?

IDEA

INTERPRET
IDEAS TO CONCEPT

THE DESIGN CYCLE

OWN IT
AVOID REITERATING EXISTING CONCEPTS OR TRANSLATING DIRECTLY FROM YOUR SOURCE

REINTERPRET
ALLOW YOUR UNIQUE PERSPECTIVE AND CREATIVE VISION TO GUIDE YOUR PROCESS

CONCEPT

INVESTIGATE
DISREGARD NOTHING

REFLECT & QUESTION
WHO, WHAT, WHERE, WHEN, WHY?

REINVENT
NEW SILHOUETTES AND FORMS

RECOGNIZE
EMERGING DESIGN THEMES WITHIN DESIGN

DESIGN

ESTABLISH
VOICE, IDENTITY & SIGNATURE STYLE

FINALIZE
DESIGN IDEAS, FABRICATION & DETAILS

Concept / Process

concept:
— something conceived in the mind: thought, notion
— an abstract or generic idea generalized from particular instances

A concept is a developed theme that surfaces from the original idea. The designer's idea evolves from original research by further investigation of specific directional themes that emerge from the collective inspiration. This stage in a sense begins to bring order out of chaos. The process is instinctive and filled with trial and error, as ideas are re-visited repeatedly and approached from differing perspectives. The designer must move beyond the surface of things in order to produce innovative results. Don't stop at the obvious. Every option must be exhausted. Dig deeper!

Within this stage of further exploration, it is good to stop and reflect on the process thus far. The act of reflection itself is a key step that often gets overlooked by designers. Caught up in the act of 'doing' they miss the opportunity to reflect on what works and what doesn't and more importantly why, before moving on to the next phase.

Certainly, the frenetic nature of fashion design, in preparation for each season, rarely allows time for reflection. As an emerging designer, still learning to understand and develop your own process, establishing the habit of self-reflection early is important and should becomes integral to your working methods. Taking stock of where you are in your process will focus direction and produce better results.

Question everything. Ask a series of 'Who, What, Where and Why' questions throughout the process: Who is my muse? What ideas work best? Why do they work? What am I communicating with this concept? Where am I going next?

Never settle for mediocrity when excellence is around the corner. The distance between the two is measured by how much you push yourself in this middle phase and doggedly investigate every option, leaving no stone unturned.

An investigation into movement and dance, using zero-waste and sustainable methods.

Process

Brainstorming / free association	**Textile / knit development**	3D draping and construction
Mind mapping	**Zero-waste flat pattern**	Fabric manipulation
Music / Dance	**2D sketching**	Zero-waste cutting
Video	**3D draping**	Textile innovation
2D painting	**Surface textile design**	Ethics
Photography	**Self-editing**	Sustainable practice
Doodling	**Recycling**	
Surface print design		

Hope for the Future

Janelle Abbott

On pages 20–25, we saw how Janelle used dance and music to kick-start the creative process, creating drapes that sought to capture movement in motion.

How, what, where, when and why?

During the next phase in her process Janelle focused more on knit development (conceptualizing and creating samples) and textile manipulation (painting fabric), but also developing a colour story, and considering how to create zero-waste markers out of some of her sketches from the previous stage.

Each week I would find myself stuck on at least one look. There was a specific dress I couldn't get away from ... The next week it was a vest with a painted and quilted fabric treatment. **Janelle Abbott**

Don't discard anything!

In the initial stages when Janelle listened to the song by Sufjan Stevens in her bedroom, its twenty-five minutes of play time gave her the opportunity to become immersed in the atmosphere created by the song and to truly absorb the various levels that pulsed within the music. Using black and white acrylics, she had painted her automatic response to the music. The paintings were a chaotic mash, but Janelle identified four particular actions, initiated by the music, that she then catalogued and assembled into a reference book.

During this particular period of exploration, Janelle visited the Sonia Delaunay exhibition at the Cooper-Hewitt National Design Museum in New York. This research, combined with Janelle's own identification of the four brush strokes, prompted her to start designing prints and fabric treatments, including embroidery and quilting that had an exotic flair, with faces that verged on kabuki and geometric patterns with a nod to futurism.

Janelle also continued her exploration of the effects of motion on silhouette. With the thought of 'capturing motion in a moment' in mind, she began to develop knitwear samples that would mimic the suspension of the garments.

One week her assignment required her to bring in 40 ideas, so she simply took 40 small squares of muslin and sewed each in a different way in order to attempt to capture the fabric in a moment of motion. This simple act of creation, and forward motion, helped Janelle to process the work she had done, simply by taking her mind off it: 'Sometimes, I find that I must do things that seem to be completely unrelated to the work at hand, in order to refresh or revise the work I have already completed. The next week I went back to my instructor with edits of both my designs and my textiles. They had a freshness of cognition that when caught "in the thick of things" is difficult to obtain, so this is why taking productive breaks is a huge necessity within my own practice.'

1

1

Brush stroke development
Janelle had identified four distinct brush strokes in her response to the music. After visiting a Sonia Delaunay exhibition, these developed into more geometric marks and were used for experimenting with embroidery and quilting.

2 / 3 / 4

Exploring motion
Janelle had also observed existing clothes in motion. She began to develop knitwear samples and sewing techniques to further develop ideas of form and silhouette.

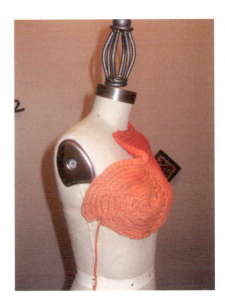
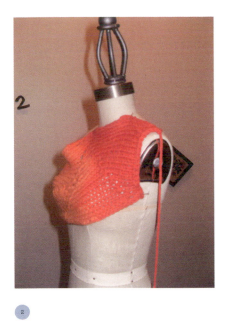
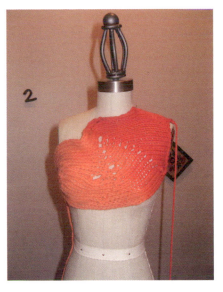

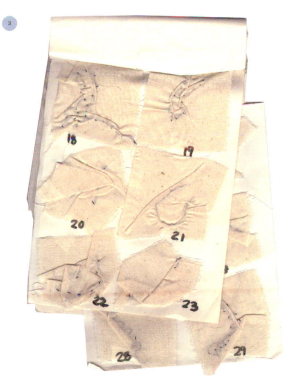

Allow your own unique perspective and creative vision to guide your process

Janelle allowed the concept of motion to infiltrate her entire approach to process, but while she allowed everything to enter into her work, she didn't allow everything to remain.

The nature of her research to this point encouraged Janelle to take a more 'artistic' approach to 'self-editing', rather than one of 'traditional design'.

The artistic approach is methodical, much like the designer's technique. But for the artist, less importance is placed on precision, and more emphasis is channelled towards productivity. It's about amassing as much work as possible. There is a point of self-editing, when you must make those 'yes' 'no' decisions within this approach, but in the face of tradition, the decisions are not made relative to one another, but relative to you: what you feel must stay and what must go. The artistic lens is self-reflexive, it focuses on the voice of the artist, whereas the designer's thought process perhaps rarely escapes considering the work in and of itself.

Working on loose-leaf sheets of paper, rescued from recycling bins around campus, Janelle used paper that had been stepped on, stapled together then ripped apart, dripping with house paint, and scribbled on. There was nothing sacred to the work Janelle was amassing. The work itself had a motion that could not be bothered by precision: 'In this manner, I felt in a sense that the work was finding itself more than I was finding it. I left the channel open wide enough that my creativity acted more as the conductor of the product than the product being a result of my creativity.'

5

6

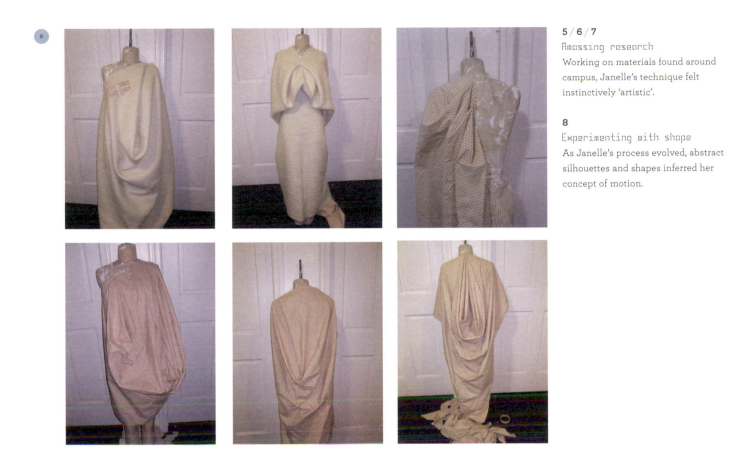

5 / 6 / 7
Amassing research
Working on materials found around campus, Janelle's technique felt instinctively 'artistic'.

8
Experimenting with shape
As Janelle's process evolved, abstract silhouettes and shapes inferred her concept of motion.

Avoid reiterating existing concepts or directly translating from your source

While Janelle began her process from existing garments worn during her dance performance, these became invisible as the process evolved, morphing into re-imagined abstract silhouettes and shapes that inferred her concept of motion and that of 'capturing motion in a garment'. In this way, she was able to take an existing form and move it forward. Her own garments acted as tools that led her towards a new way of seeing clothes within the wider context of the connections between dance, drawing and fashion, under the umbrella theme of 'motion'.

Sifting through everything that had been amassed throughout the process, it was clear that the completed designs strongly referenced the stills pulled from the dance performance series and the automatic painting that had been spurred on by the initial song.

It is interesting to note that while Janelle's process may appear to be random initially – a somewhat organized chaos, in the final analysis it reflects a simultaneous linear methodology.

Turn to page 20 to see PART I (Idea) of this project, or page 148 for PART III (Design).

A collection based on culture and social processes, from garment design to presentation.

Process

Observational research	**2D visualization**	3D construction
Narrative	**Fashion cultural reference**	Brainstorming
Digital technology	**3D deconstruction**	2D / 3D visualization
Brainstorming	**2D collage**	Digital technical flat drawing
2D sketching	**Narrative**	2D editing
Journaling	**3D draping**	Exhibition
Digital collage	**Colour / fabrication**	
Exhibition	**2D flat pattern**	

Virtual Appropriation
Melitta Baumeister

On pages 26–31, we saw how Melitta had explored appropriation art to play with the idea of reuse in design and presentation.

How, what, where, when and why?

In this next phase of the process, Melitta moved the concept of appropriation forward by creating 'couples' (one design that is 'copying' the other in a certain way). She saw this as a continuation of developing form and worked with copies or 'couples' of designs mostly within the inner lines and garment details. This enabled her to see the act of 'copying' as a way to reach an ideal of form or design. She also created groups in colour to further explore the concept.

The act of 'copying' in fashion is an accepted part of the fashion system. The trickle-down effect from designer to street fashion is partly what sustains the business itself. For a design to become a 'fashion trend' it must be widely accepted by the mass market. Melitta is curious about these types of facts that exist within our fashion culture and in this instance this reality informed her process and approach within this project as she co-opted this macro function on a micro level.

Melitta's design process was ongoing and parallel to the photographs she worked into sketches in her research book. The process varied between 2D visualization and 3D forms. In the creation of the 3D component, Melitta worked in a variety of ways: either working with a quarter-scale dress form, where she explored shape by draping with fabric, or she deconstructed existing garments. She documented each step of the process by taking photographs. These then helped in the development of the 3D constructions and silhouettes.

As a designer, where it is relevant to her work, Melitta reflects on society and her observations of daily life and utilizes these concepts within her collections. By observing the virtual world that most people interact with daily and reacting to its impact on the real world, its surface or loss of tangible surface, Melitta summarizes these thoughts and allows this narrative to drive the design for her collection forward. She deconstructs the habits of society. What began as an idea first exhibited within the 'copy/paste' function in Part I, or via the concept of believing in something that is merely a simulation, now becomes translated into clothing.

1

1 / 2 / 3 / 4
Sketchbook work
Melitta developed her theme through
drawings and photographs in her
sketchbook. She experimented with
'couples', copying designs between
them, continuing the reappropriation
theme.

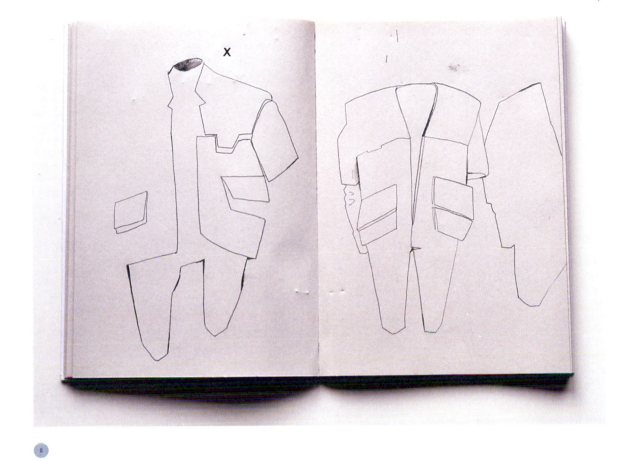

2

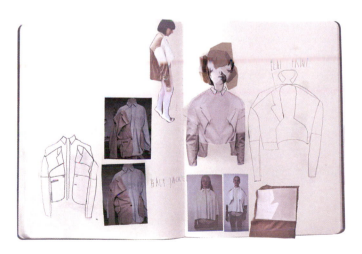

3

4

Don't discard anything!

Melitta created a series of 3D toiles using existing second-hand garments. For example, she cut up a men's suit and used only the pieces that she needed, such as a lapel or shoulder parts with sleeves. This was another form of deconstruction similar to that done on the computer with foreign material.

Melitta began to work out the details and interpretation within her initial concept. Through print development and seam detailing, she translated virtual aesthetics such as flatness and disembodiment into fashion design ideas. She then projected her own designs that had been developed digitally, onto a dress form to discover the lines, proportions and dimensions of the garments and to be able to imagine them in 3D. She used digital technology to bring the 2D image into 3D reality.

Melitta defined the concept from the following keywords:

Virtual aesthetic: flatness of what the form was previously (for example, the second-hand clothing), translated via a non-tangible simulation of shapes and form that are now printed or stitched onto the surface of the garment to represent the virtual world.

Disembodiment: shapes that are empty/disembodied (for example, the pieces Melitta used from the deconstructed garments) represented in seam lines on the new designs.

Copy/paste: reuse of the same idea (for example, existing shapes through repeated lines).

Ready-made: as a design base (copies from existing material or existing garments).

From these she developed her details: surface, fabric manipulation and finishing.

Lastly, Melitta transferred colours from her moodboards. These were later developed into four main colour groups within the collection, in the form of a digital colour scale; from warm light brown through to white to grey to dark brown. Each scale morphs from one group within the collection to another.

Allow your own unique perspective and creative vision to guide your process

While working on her project, Melitta had noticed a number of empty shops in her local area. Drawn to these empty spaces, she decided she'd like to use one to exhibit her collection and make the translation from computer screen to real life. Melitta had one particular shop window in mind; it had been free for over a year. Having contacted the landlord with her proposal, he replied to say that he would be happy to offer the space to her for free.

This provided Melitta with the opportunity to work not only on her collection itself, but also on the presentation of her work. This was conceptually very important to her. The offer of a free space provided an opportunity to collaborate and helped her think further about her concept. It opened up many possibilities to think about how she could express herself to the world as a designer. She called this process 'space appropriation' (the act of making a public space your own): 'People use places to meet up which are not intended for that purpose; for example, by projecting onto the wall of a building the user takes ownership of it for that time period and imprints his own vision onto it.'

In Melitta's case, the act of taking over an empty store for her exhibition was her own interpretation of making a space your own and not what it was before. The empty shop window was not empty anymore, and therefore changed: 'By changing a shop window you change the street, and people's perception of it.'

5
Detail development
Detail samples allowed Melitta to experiment with texture, colour and finishing.

Avoid reiterating existing concepts or directly translating from your source

In Melitta's case, her entire concept was built on deconstructing existing concepts and making them her own. By reappropriating forms, silhouettes, details, physical space and virtual space, she forced us to rethink the space 'in between' reality and the virtual world. Her original shapes were derived from menswear, but then reappropriated into womenswear. Melitta then projected these digitally deconstructed images she had developed onto her dress form to create new reconstructed 3D forms of her own design.

Melitta worked in an original way by taking what is a traditionally a 3D process (draping) and 2D process (flat pattern-making) and combined them within a digital format to create new silhouettes. She utilized technology to navigate between these various ways of working to reimagine silhouette and form within the context of her concept. The final result at this stage is her ability to take a digital design and make it real.

Turn to page 26 to see PART I (Idea) of this project, or page 154 for PART III (Design).

Textile innovation driven by an investigation into what lies beneath the skin.

Process

2D visualization	**2D visualization**	Self-reflection
Narrative	**3D draping**	Textile innovation
Textile exploration	**2D flat pattern**	3D draping
Hand craft	**Printing technology**	Sustainable practice
Embroidery	**Textile surface design**	Technology
Knitting		Collaboration
Digital technology		Hand craft
		Editorial photography

Neurovision

Jovana Mirabile

On pages 32–37, we saw how Jovana researched a number of body imaging techniques and dyeing methods to generate a number of print designs.

How, what, where, when and why?

Here, Jovana interpreted these questions within the context of customer and environment. While the initial idea was clear, how to translate and then execute this into a collection was not. In order to help define a direction, the concept of a muse was explored by collecting a variety of images that would identify the customer's lifestyle (interiors, lighting, colour and editorial images). By exploring who 'she' might be, what 'she' would wear, and where 'she' would wear it, a more clearly defined ideal emerged in the form of a glamorous, enigmatic persona. A saturated, neon colour palette derived from the prints dictated the bold personality of both the muse and, subsequently, the collection.

Design should be a fully rounded exercise in visual stimulation, intellectual interpretation, 2D representation and 3D realization. **Jovana Mirabile**

Don't discard anything!

It is crucial to exhaust every option and push ideas as far as possible. In this particular process, Jovana employed a variety of approaches: 3D draping with paper on the dress form, zero-waste pattern-making, photography, 2D sketching and back to 3D draping. Moving back and forth between these methods enabled Jovana to see the design process from new perspectives, and an idea gains momentum when seen from a variety of vantage points.

A threefold linear framework was evident in the 3D draping process: the draping on the dress form itself, photographing the drapes, and then tracing over the photographs to create new ideas. Silhouettes were then developed with more detail in the sketchbook. At this point in the process, each new design formed a modified version of the previous iteration and key elements were carried forward. Zero-waste pattern-cutting techniques informed 3D development by starting with one yard (90cm) of fabric and exploring shapes on the dress form without cutting. Seeking to highlight the wholeness of the body, Jovana chose to completely eliminate side seams. This was achieved by draping on the bias and creating bias tubes, which where then draped on the form automatically.

After the 3D phase, Jovana started to develop key design details in 2D and began pairing individual items together in head-to-toe looks. At this point in the 2D sketch phase, attention was paid to the mixing of prints, colours, knits, and embroideries, along with a consideration of how the inside of the garments could reflect the concept of the body beneath the skin. This led to the idea of reversibility.

1 / 2 / 3

Exploring mood, colour and a muse

Jovana used the concept of a muse to move her ideas forward. By examining who this might be, a more clearly defined ideal emerged.

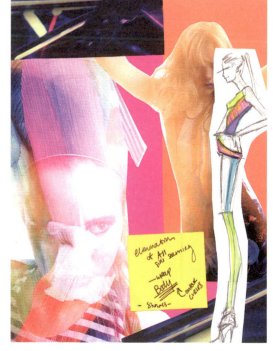

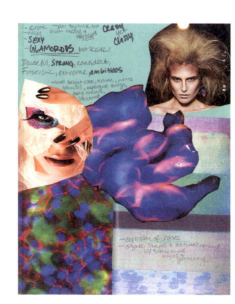

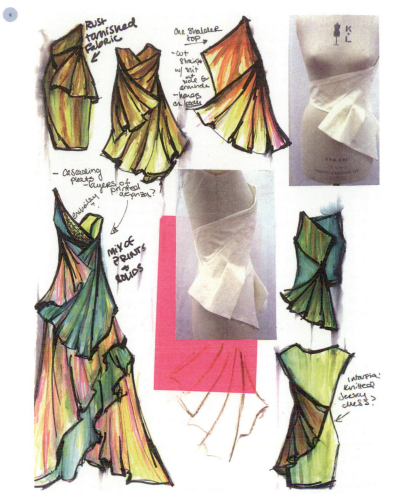

4 / 5 / 6 / 7
3D drape, photograph and sketch
Jovana moved between 2D and 3D
to play with flat pattern, photography
and draping. This enabled her to
play with ideas of print, colour, knit,
embroidery and zero-waste
techniques.

Allow your own unique
perspective and creative
vision to guide your process

The concept of technology was an underlying theme that had emerged from the onset in this project. In tandem with this was the designer's growing personal desire to utilize sustainable methods, when possible, within the design process. As a result of a sponsorship opportunity, the final four print designs were selected to be created by AirDye® (a waterless printing technology), which would provide an ecologically viable solution to the printing process. This is a great example of collaboration. These sponsored opportunities provided Jovana with the opportunity to work in ways she could not have accomplished alone. With this new technology, the neon-saturated colours of the textiles were brought to life and the potential for reversibility and minimal waste was enhanced thanks to the double-sided AirDye® printing technique that no longer required linings.

8 / 9 / 10 / 11
Print and surface techniques
New technology provided Jovana with
an ecologically viable solution to the
printing process.

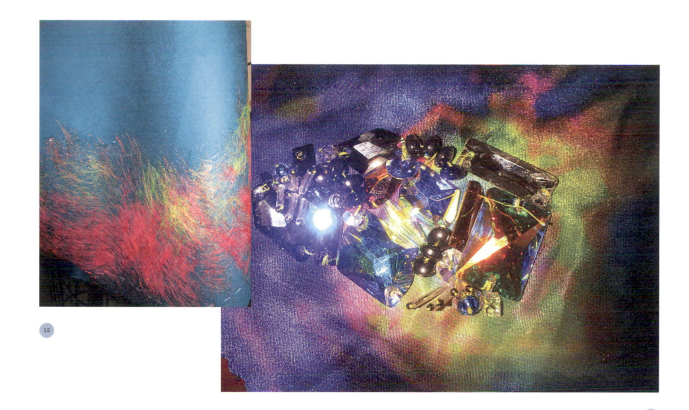

Avoid reiterating existing concepts or directly translating from your source

At this final concept development stage, more experimentation was done with different yarns in neon colours, using fusible Angelina® fibre, which provides an iridescent colour when bonded to itself through the application of heat. Samples were made by bonding fibre to felted wool and knits, along with needle felting, which resulted in an ombré blend of Angelina® fibres. One of the prints was converted to a knit jacquard, introducing texture into the collection. Design decisions were not made at this point since the 3D process would be key to the development of this phase.

Remaining within the textile development realm, the initial idea was moved beyond a literal interpretation of the cells as print into a more nuanced translation of subtle fibre techniques, along with a variety of hand- and machine-knits. The choice to delay finalizing designs until the 3D draping stage was key at this stage, as this left room for continued experimentation.

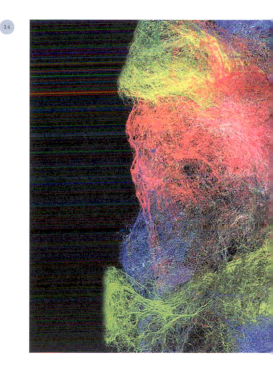

12 / 13 / 14
Experimenting with yarns
Fibres were felted and fused, bonded and embellished to create a more nuanced translation of the vibrant cell images.

Turn to page 32 to see PART I (Idea) of this project, or page 160 for PART III (Design).

A reinvention of traditional craft techniques to create new textiles and garments

Process

Research	**Textile development**	'Knitted' textile development
2D visualization	**Digital technology**	Materiality
Fabric manipulation	**3D development**	3D draping
Craft techniques	**Craft technique**	Photography
Textile research	**3D form**	Editorial direction
Materiality	**2D visualization**	2D visual narration
3D digital draping	**Materiality**	Film
Photography	**Textile innovation**	
Technical drawing	**3D textile / draping**	
3D draping		

Knitting and Pleating

Jie Li

On pages 38–43, we saw how Jie played with strips of fabric on the dress form, knitting and pleating them to experiment with shape and texture.

How, what, where, when and why?

After the initial stage of investigating the craft, via research, materials and working on the form in 3D, Jie next had to make some decisions about what worked and what had not. Through her testing of the various shapes and pleat techniques, she had decided that the accordion worked best.

The repetition of knitting led her to work further with the mirror-imaging technique in Adobe Photoshop to recreate the actual garment shapes themselves. She wondered if she pleated a very long piece of fabric what would happen at the bottom. She did a quick drawing of this idea and then began attempting to pleat this by hand. This proved very difficult due to the volume of fabric, so Jie sourced a local factory that could do this for her and sent the fabric out to be pleated.

She moved further into 3D development, combining the pleated fabric in pineapple, accordion and side pleats, while she continued to develop her own handcrafted versions along with the crochet. All three together provided variety in texture and proportion and the initial idea of craft technique had come full circle as the process now included machine-made and handmade fabrics in a new way: 'I recognize how this has been done historically but this is now how I do it. This project challenged me to address the most fundamental of elements when designing a collection, that of craft, technique, and make. I used pleating and knitting to create my garment in a new way, which I practised and eventually reinvented into a contemporary fashion context, building silhouette through the craft of knit and pleat.'

For Jie, design happens in the process of investigating fabrics and within the technical drawings she created to remember the process, stitches and the pattern of the 'knitting'. The process started with the 3D form then moved to Adobe Photoshop and into a 2D visualization. In this manner, Jie was able to see the actual garment and design versus an imagined one.

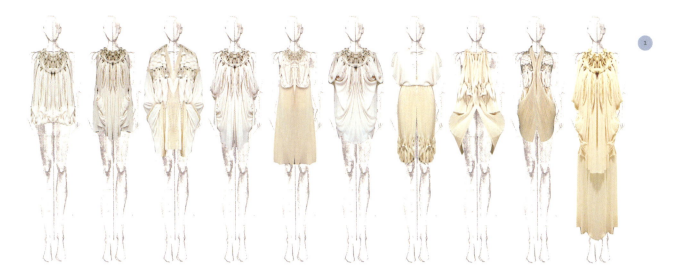

Don't discard anything!

Finally, Jie decided to use the accordion pleat and visited some pleating companies. They could make different sizes so she needed to do some fabric tests. At this stage, Jie worked diligently to test a variety of fabrics and discovered that silk and cotton made an accordion pleat easily. She made different widths of pleats: three inches, two inches and one inch wide by one-and-a-half yards long, with about five or six pleats deep (similar to her very first experiment). These were her 'yarn' for 'knitting'. Jie then linked them together to create a very long strand and wound these into balls. She also mixed different types of fabric pleats together to create an original multi-textured 'yarn'. This comprised three silk pleats and three cotton pleats that were then fused together. Jie liked the effect of thick pleats supporting soft pleats within one fabric.

Allow your own unique perspective and creative vision to guide your process

After the experience of working on the dress form, Jie started to knit full pieces, mixing all the various techniques and combining all she had learned to create a new knit fabric. She allowed her own unique perspective and creative vision to guide her process, making these swatches big enough to cover the torso from neck to waist. Finally, she used her 'yarn' to link these together. There is no paper pattern for this garment, it is created by hand 'knitting' and working with the pleated fabric only.

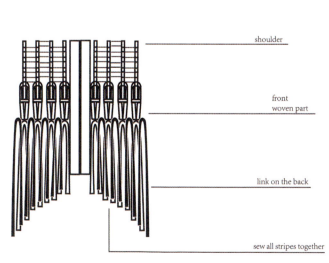

shoulder

front
woven part

link on the back

sew all stripes together

1 / 2 / 3
Photoshop and 2D visualization
Jie used sketching and Adobe Photoshop to create different garment shapes, before trying them out by hand.

4

Pleating techniques
Jie tested various pleating techniques
to further explore her ideas.

5 / 6 / 7 / 8

Hand Knitting on the dress form
Each piece was developed individually
by draping or 'knitting' the fabric on
the dress form.

Avoid reiterating existing
concepts or directly
translating from your source

While Jie utilized existing crafts, she moved them forward in a new way by bringing a traditional technique into a new innovative form that drives silhouette. The technique is complex but it is the foundation for the design of the garment itself. Each piece is developed individually by draping or 'knitting' the fabric on the form itself, creating new forms.

When she began research for the project, Jie was very aware of the iconic influence of Issey Miyake and his signature pleating within his collections. She was keen to use pleating in a different way. By creating her own version of a pleat with combinations of different fabrications and the technique of 'knitting', Jie successfully accomplished this.

5

6

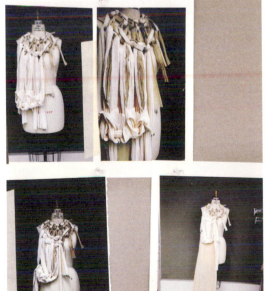

7

6

Functional separates, designed for longevity and adaptation.

Process

Video	**Problem solving**	Self-reflection
2D sketching	**Technical flat sketching**	Journaling
Brainstorming	**Visual merchandising**	Final editing
List making		2D styling
Journaling	**Designing 'piece-by-piece'**	Knitwear development
Textile development	**Design editing and research**	Flat sketching
Colour	**Textile development**	Fabrication
Silhouette	**Journaling**	2D final presentation
Customization	**Narrative**	

Growth and Decay

Andrea Tsao

On pages 44–49, we saw how Andrea was inspired to investigate notions of permanence and personalization in clothing.

How, what, where, when and why?

Carried over from the idea stage was Andrea's challenge of how to create a collection that reflected the work of sculptor Andy Goldsworthy yet embraced her own concept. Her idea of creating clothing that was adjustable for a fluctuating body size, and taking into consideration the wear and tear of a garment were good starting points, but solving how this would play out in reality within the design context, without seeming contrived, was a tough call: 'Moving from an intellectually abstract concept to a design concept is always the toughest bridge to build. Garments are garments, but there must always be a reason for each particular detail (this is essentially how I stay away from creating things that seem contrived).

In order to focus her mind on a collection centred on the concept of the permanence of clothing, Andrea felt it important to address the specific details and design elements of each garment. Instead of sketching in the traditional manner (head-to-toe looks on a figure), Andrea decided to work with technical flat sketches, showing back and side views as well as fronts, thinking about each piece individually rather than the overall look they would create. This method of designing meant that the collection would be more piece-driven and therefore more flexible and thus consistent with the aesthetic Andrea was attempting to create.

For Andrea, this collection was not about each look, but about the items that made each look up, for a number of reasons. Goldsworthy himself often had to make do with the surroundings he was working amongst and the tools that nature supplied him. He had to reorder them in a way that was deliberate, calculated, and at the same time spontaneous. Also, a piece-driven collection reinforced the idea of permanence within a garment. 'We, as consumers, splurge on items we think we get the most value from, and the biggest deciding factor is determined by a garment's projected lifespan. If a garment has the potential to be worn in a flattering way despite changes to your body, changes in trends, or the wear and tear on the garment, doesn't this make the piece more valuable? I really wanted to create a collection with individual pieces representing this level of value.'

Don't discard anything!

At this stage, Andrea didn't want to rid herself of any of Goldsworthy's imagery. She selected fabric swatches of textures that reminded her of his work, picked up trims that she found beautiful – even if not necessarily relevant at that moment – and pasted them into her sketchbook for reference.

Her goal was to capture the moment and investigate the potential for silhouette change using drawstrings. She wanted to create dramatic shapes in her sketches that embodied how she felt about Goldsworthy's work and its graphic, emotional, natural, and fragile quality. Andrea worked in earthy tones and incessant layering of different garments. She compared Goldsworthy's method of working with the blank palette of nature to her own method of working with the blank palette of the body. His approach to creating sculpture and art by layering elements one on top of another now paralleled her own; his action of building art was now mimicked in her design approach as she pulled and tugged at the drawstrings in an effort to manipulate the fabric into new desirable shapes.

1 / 2 / 3

Inspiration and reference
Throughout this stage, Andrea was careful to keep Goldsworthy in mind. She selected fabric swatches that reminded her of his work and created dramatic shapes that embodied how she felt about his art.

Allow your own unique perspective and creative vision to guide your process

Andrea is very self-aware and understands her design proclivities. She loves textured fabrics, vibrant colours, prints and the use of trims, cording and embellishments such as beading and embroidery. She typically layers garments on top of one another to create a look. In short, she is not a minimalist! Her strength as a designer lies in separates (particularly jackets), accessories and trousers (often the bane of every design student's existence!). She believes in a beautifully detailed trouser along with a perfect sweater. Keeping some of this in mind and reminding herself not to be repetitive, she realized there was no place in this collection for too many bright colours and that beading and embroidery were not relevant. Based on the original inspiration and the elements that drove her design ideas at the onset of her process, she recognized that this was a down-to-earth, free-form collection, and the additional design details she had used previously were not consistent with her concept in this instance. She made the choice to allow colour vibrancy to manifest in oranges, ambers, and greens for a spring/summer collection.

These choices are key. Whilst still acknowledging her own vision as a designer, Andrea allowed the specifics of this particular inspiration to direct her decisions on every level: silhouette, details, finishing, colour palette and choice of season.

Avoid reiterating existing concepts or directly translating from your source

From the outset, Andrea set out to avoid reiterating her typical ways of working and used this as inspiration to take her in a new direction, both conceptually and within the context of her design aesthetic and silhouettes:

'Up to this point, I hadn't really been able to take an inspiration and apply the intellectual details behind the original idea to my own work, developing it to a point where there is an entirely new concept. Sure, this project is about Andy Goldsworthy, but it is really about the permanence of clothing, and questioning that notion. My collection certainly captures the autumnal warmth of some of his work, and maintains the fragile yet beautiful mood of his sculptures, but the collection has developed a mind of its own. It is a concept in its own right, and it took deep exploration in order for me to reach this point.

I think that when many students begin to design, it is all about visual, tangible inspiration. This collection marked a turning point for me in my journey as a student. It wasn't about finding a picture of something I liked and emulating the details from that picture. Instead, it was about an intangible concept and how it manifested itself in my brain and subsequently onto the page. This influenced my working method from this point onwards, and I began approaching each new project in a similar way. My inspirations since have been intangible concepts with an exploration of the intellectual and scientific, and whatever else I consider to be beautiful. To me, a sculpture is more beautiful once I comprehend the reasoning behind its creation and the interpretation of what it is. This project encouraged me to take a different approach to research, to continue being inspired by thought processes, social phenomena, literary text, and history.'

4 / 5 / 6
Piece by piece development
Andrea found that she preferred working on her collection piece by piece.

From a process point of view, this was the first time Andrea had worked with materials she was bound to, using dyes and colours she had created herself. She again referenced Goldsworthy's method of working – he would spend hours trying to prop up one leaf against another, working only with what was around him, so Andrea too would stay true to her colour palette and the fabrics she herself developed.

At this point, Andrea was certain of what she wanted from the process. Her vision became clearer the more she wrote in her book. Some of the most important phrases that she carried from beginning to end were:

1. Growth/Staying/Decay

2. Natural change: unpredictability and volatility, un-editable raw materials, fragility and delicacy, and limited means.

3. Balance and putting shapes together to create a whole. Allowing things to happen naturally.

4. Customization: Taking these un-editable raw materials and allowing the wearer to edit them according to the natural shape of their body and the wear and tear of their lives.

5. Delicate but powerful images; silhouettes that are dramatic and speak volumes, but also with a delicate quality. For example, if the silhouette is strong and dramatic, the straps on the dress are quarter-inch thin and look barely strong enough to hold up the dress. Similarly, the drawstrings that encircle cut-outs in the garments allow for a sense of weightlessness.

These words reminded Andrea where she started, and where she wanted to go, providing a map for the journey.

Andrea was also sure of her customer and aesthetic: a tomboyish and athletic collection emerged, which, she was convinced, even women with more feminine tastes would desire. The garments would be delicate – not from embellishment but from tiny details such as shirring, drawstrings, and elastics in cut-outs (sexy but at the same time athletic). As a result of this perspective, she researched more images of street style to inform her process.

'The more I sketched, the more I realized who this customer was. She was down-to-earth, young and enjoyed making an expressive statement with her clothing. The collection is focused on personal customization, durability and ease, with a feminine yet tomboyish, aggressive attitude. The garments are worn on the street and can be easily thrown on, yet still look refined.

Clearly, designers working in the industry design with a specific customer in mind, and while it can be helpful to work in this way while in school, it can be limiting to the emerging designer who is still trying to find their own aesthetic and it might be argued that if they focus on the latter the former will follow. In Andrea's case this is intrinsic to her own method of working and informs her design process. For her it is central to her thought process and directs her understanding of the collection development.

Turn to page 44 to see part I (Idea) of this project, or page 172 for part III (Design).

Graphic imagery translated into three-dimensional silhouettes via innovative knitwear techniques.

Process

2D / 3D visualization	Idiom	2D / 3D editing
Photography	2D editing	3D sketching
3D reconstruction	3D draping	3D knit / textile innovation
3D draping	2D sketching	
3D shape / form	Textile / knit development	3D draping
	2D visualization	3D construction
	Photography	Colour / fabrication
	Digital technology	Technical knit development
	Knit innovation	Editorial photography

Trompe L'Oeil

Sara Bro-Jørgensen

On pages 50–55, we saw how Sara played with abstract photography to inform experiments in layered fabric and new shapes.

How, what, where, when and why?

In this next phase, Sara began to develop the abstract photographs into a design language. Her stylistic expression emerged as she turned an abstract 2D image into a coherent 3D collection reflecting both the style and mood of the original images.

She divided the images into the following groups: shapes, textiles, atmosphere and pattern. This was quite a tricky phase for Sara: she was working on all aspects of the collection at the same time, drawing from her ideas randomly without knowing where it would take her. This meant that she often had to step back and look at the process, editing samples and drawings and putting some aside for later or saving for other projects. This is an extremely important practice to follow. It is often difficult to think of reusing a previously discarded idea from another collection, but returning to it at a later date may bring fresh perspectives on how to approach it.

Editing is a particularly challenging task for most designers; they can become very attached to specific designs or details. Students during the early stages of design development often make poor choices. Either they pile all their favourite ideas into one outfit, or they combine key pieces that worked together originally but don't necessarily work in their new combinations. It is a delicate balance of developing an instinct for simply knowing what works within a collection and what doesn't. Developing this instinct takes time, and is gained from much trial and error and, most importantly, by learning from mistakes!

Sara continued to work using a variety of methods simultaneously: 3D draping, 2D sketching and knit development. She started out by developing some knitted swatches and using these for 3D draping. This gave her an idea of how to change the knitting technique to make it work with the shape. She then sketched her ideas to get the proportions right. In this way she would move back and forth between the different methods, revising the design until she was satisfied with the results.

Sara traced some of the shapes from the graphic images she had captured, and these later became the basis for large-scale graphic jacquard knits and garment shapes. First, she simply traced lines from the image, then changed the scale and proportion; some lines became thicker, some thinner. She then mirrored the image in order for it to work as a pattern on the body. This process was very methodical and systematic in its approach: Sara was essentially taking the graphic images and refining them until she was satisfied with the desired visual effect.

Pattern development

1

Two-colour jacquard
This knit method made the image
appear very graphic.

2

'Blistering' method
The 'blistering' knit method made the
image appear softer and less graphic.

Don't discard anything!

During the next phase, Sara used 3D draping to play with scale and the placement of the graphic patterns on the body. Here, she discovered that by using different knitting techniques, she could make one pattern look completely different. A two-coloured knit jacquard made the image appear very graphic, whereas a 'blistered' knit technique made the image appear softer and less graphic. (Both techniques were carried out on a digital knitting machine.)

Sara also used 3D draping to experiment with shape. She photographed fabric draped on the dress form and then collaged these photographs in new ways to create innovative shapes.

This process was very useful. Designers often sketch designs from their imagination; they have no real point of reference. In this case, Sara had the advantage of working in the reverse; she draped the silhouettes on the dress form and then worked in 2D to put these together into looks for the development of the collection.

(3)

3

Collaged garments
Sara collaged photographs on the dress form to experiment with shape.

4

Textile innovation
Sara combined and contrasted materials such as heavy knits, sheer chiffon and leather.

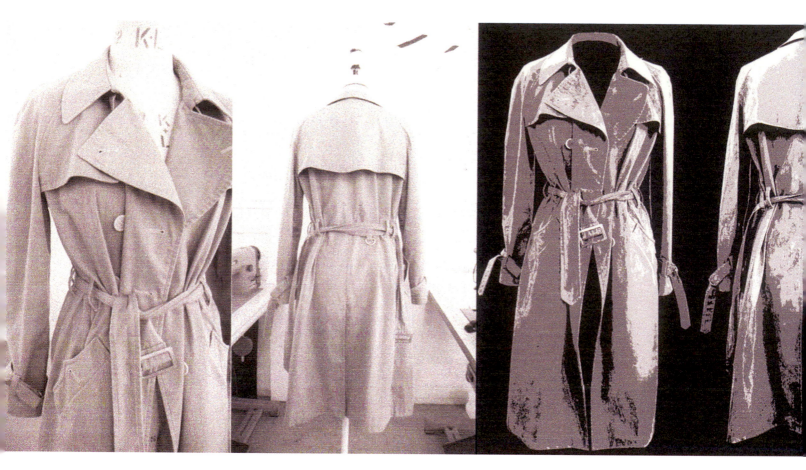

Allow your own unique perspective and creative vision to guide your process

Sara's background in textiles and her experience as a knitwear designer strongly influenced her way of working. At the start, she was very much centred on fabric and the development of new knitting techniques. She swatched first and then based her shapes on the textile's qualities. This project was typical of Sara's approach: 'I've always been interested in combining and contrasting ideas, shapes and patterns. Combining something very feminine with something graphic and masculine, for example. Or heavy, thick knit with thin, sheer fabrics; boxy graphic shapes with draped asymmetrical silhouettes and decorated pieces with minimalistic clean shapes. I guess it's about finding the balance between two opposites or contrasts by combining them and making them into one expression.'

5

Photograph to knit
Sara liked the idea of using photography as the basis for her patterns, so she started experimenting with photographs of iconic garments. Here she takes a photograph of a trench coat and converts it into a pattern that could be produced on a knitting machine.

6

Fitting and working on shape
By draping the fabric, Sara was then able to work on the shape of the garment.

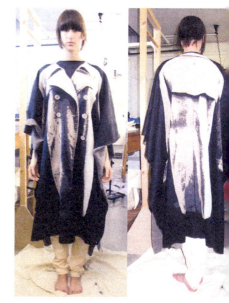

5

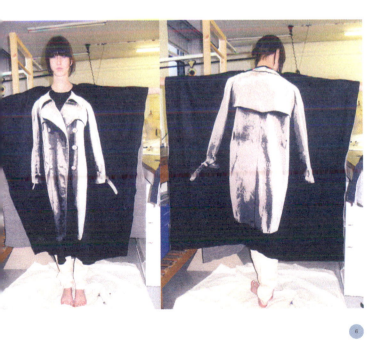

6

Avoid reiterating existing concepts or directly translating from your source

Sara developed knitted samples that reflected the key qualities of her initial inspiration. She translated the thick and thin graphic lines into chunky hand-knits, combined with layers of thin silk tulle. Here we see the connections again being made between 2D and 3D processes in a holistic approach to design. Sara was constantly moving back and forth through these spheres and in this instance was making connections from 2D imagery to 3D materiality.

She combined and contrasted materials such as heavy knit, sheer, fine chiffon and leather, and attached shredded silk tulle to knitted samples, creating long fringes or using silver chains to make embroidery on perforated leather.

The idea of using photographic imagery as a basis for her patterns, both in an abstract way and in a more literal way, intrigued Sara so she began photographing everyday iconic garments such as trench coats, jeans and T-shirts. As a result, Sara decided to use these in a literal translation, as images on the garments, playing with 2D and 3D effects and eventually achieving the look she wanted by turning them into a four-colour knit jacquard pattern. She first took a picture of the garment, then via the computer reduced the colours of the image down to four, and changed the size of the file so that one pixel on the screen would equal one stitch on the knitting machine. Sara then transferred the file to the knitting machine to convert it into a knitting pattern in order to create the fabric.

Sara then started working with the patterns individually, taking selected samples and jacquard patterns one by one and draping on a dress form to create shapes that worked for each technique. The knitted samples and the jacquards she had developed created shapes that reflected her starting point: the photographs.

3D draping is an important part of Sara's design process as all the fabrics she uses are original knits that she has designed and made. This means that more often than not it is the fabric that dictates the shape rather than Sara deciding on a shape and then selecting the right fabric to create the silhouette.

Turn to page 50 to see PART I (Idea) of this project, or page 178 for PART III (Design).

Experiments in new technology and materials.

Process

Social media research	**3D draping**	3D drape
2D photography	**Textile development**	Editing
2D flat pattern	**Wearable technology**	Collaboration
Repurposing	**Fabric innovation**	Textile development
Collaboration	**3D construction**	3D construction / innovation
	3D experimentation	Self-reflection
		2D collage

121

'Light Painting' by Leah Mendelson

PART I
Idea / Practice
56

PART II
Concept/Practice

PART III
Design / Practice
184

Light Painting
Leah Mendelson

On pages 56–61, we saw how Leah photographed light to create drapes and shapes on the human form.

How, what, where, when and why?

The original context of the project initially prompted Leah to approach Beene's sense of graphic geometry by creating amorphous shapes. She allowed this to evolve into a more graphic 'foam' drape in this concept stage. Within the 3D draping, she did a lot of direct cutting and tucking, essentially creating darts to create new shapes and silhouettes, then used markers to design her textile directly on top.

Now that Leah had clothing to work with, she wanted to create a direct connection with the initial light painting. Her goal was to bring the real essence of light to the clothes. A few months earlier she took a wearable technology class that introduced her to EL paper (a thin, flexible sheet of light-up plastic that can be laser-cut and battery-operated), and she decided to apply this material to her process.

Within the draping process, Leah discovered by mistake that she could peel off a layer of netting to reveal the raw foam underneath.

Leah adopted this 'discovery' into her draping process and peeled off the netting layer of foam, placing it in between the transparencies of her photographs with the EL paper behind it to light up the graphics of her textiles. The netting had a twill-like texture that was further emphasized by the light. Now the actual graphics of the photos were being incorporated directly into her fabric, and being lit up.

As Leah stated from the beginning, she knew that this type of abstract project would have the potential to yield many different results design-wise. She states, 'I can't think of anything more amorphous, transient, and less grounded in 3D reality than light frozen in time.' Digital printing would have been a no-brainer, but how would she approach pattern-cutting light? Would she trace a few ribbons of light and try to construct it? Draw the outline of a light silhouette, and release it from its context of light by removing the light imagery, ending up with this odd and organic silhouette? Or she could then pattern-cut into this, with the details of pockets, lapels, or one side of a jacket digitally printed.

In the end, Leah didn't try any of these techniques. Sometimes there are simply too many options and it requires self-editing. As emerging designers gain more experience, they can enter into richer and more advanced techniques of design more quickly. Leah recognized this and that she might be better able to embrace some of these more advanced techniques at a later time.

1 / 2

Play and experimentation
Leah allowed herself plenty of time
to experiment with the photographs
from the shoot, and how they could be
applied to fabrics and garments.

Don't discard anything!

This project unfolded in three stages over the span of a year. The first incarnation was completed eight weeks after doing the light painting photo shoot. The shoot took almost two weeks to prepare, from beginning to end, which significantly cut into the design process. Leah was aware of this, but she was willing to take the risk. The result was an acceptable project, but it wasn't entirely complete. She revisited the idea in the summer, during her portfolio class, and started making abstract marker drawings, then developed textiles with markers that led to textile-based designs. The following semester, in design class Leah began the draping, transparency, and EL paper work.

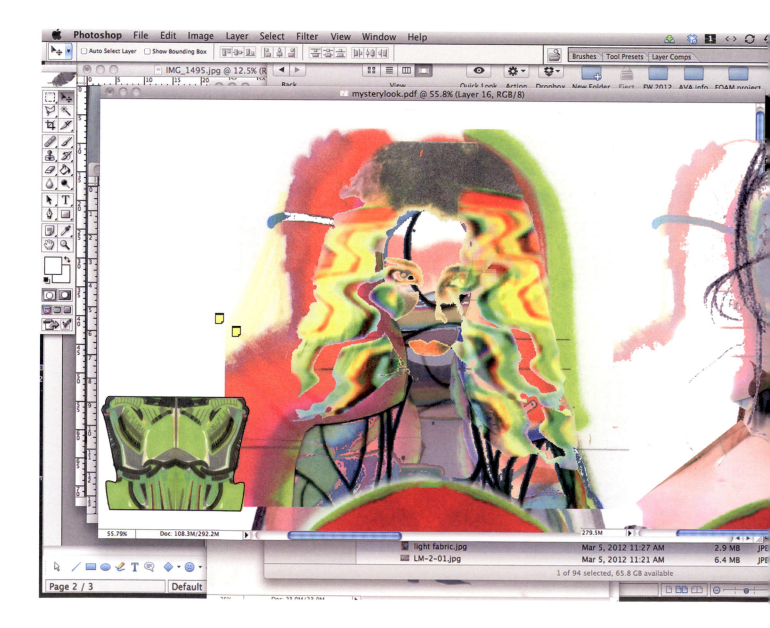

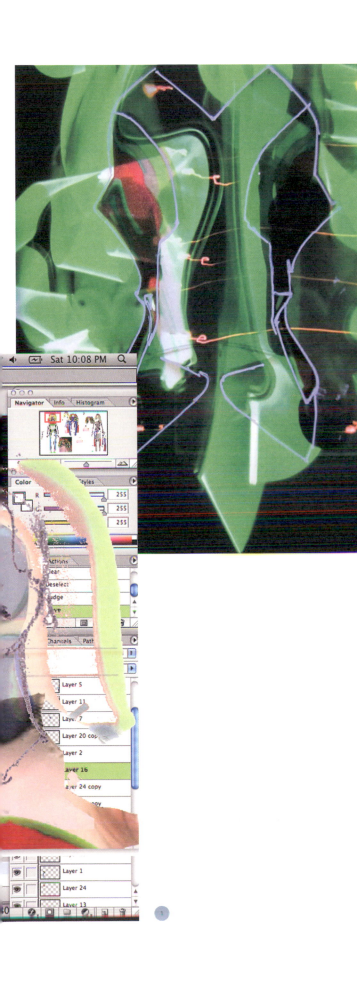

2

1

Allow your own unique perspective and creative vision to guide your process

Leah recognized that it was important to follow the research process; she saw this as a time of play and experimentation. She allowed herself to remain open and not limit herself by assuming where she would end up. She tried several different techniques to develop design ideas for this project. She did some 2D sketch design development. Then she used some photos of a jersey jumpsuit she had sewn previously for a friend to wear on the set of his own film. There was a large amount of seam allowance, and he had worn the suit on inside out. It was also a little small for him, so it gently pulled the seam allowance, creating tension and giving it fluid lines that reminded her of some of the lines created by the light in her photos. She incorporated this line into a suit, with a few different applications.

The idea didn't seem to gel so she decided to cut out some lines of light from her photos and put these into her design development page. She then attempted to draw designs over their organic graphic shapes. In the midst of this process, Leah took a show design class. This resulted in a small project where she literally cut out the transparencies from her photos and draped them over her foot. The idea had been to create lucite heels with a sense of poured plastic moving through them, just like the 3D flow found in glass-blown paperweights.

When working on this project, Leah really had to trust her own intuition. When she began drawing the textile straight onto the foam with markers, she didn't plan on cutting and draping it. This design of the textile was done spontaneously, sitting in the stairwell, while waiting for her friend to get home. She described the process of drawing in a childlike manner, with markers strewn all around her, without any ideas of where it was going, just enjoying what she was doing and trying to make it interesting and beautiful. She didn't consciously draw from the light painting for those marker drawings, but in retrospect she saw how they connected.

I can't think of anything more amorphous, transient, and less grounded in 3D reality than light frozen in time. **Leah Mendelson**

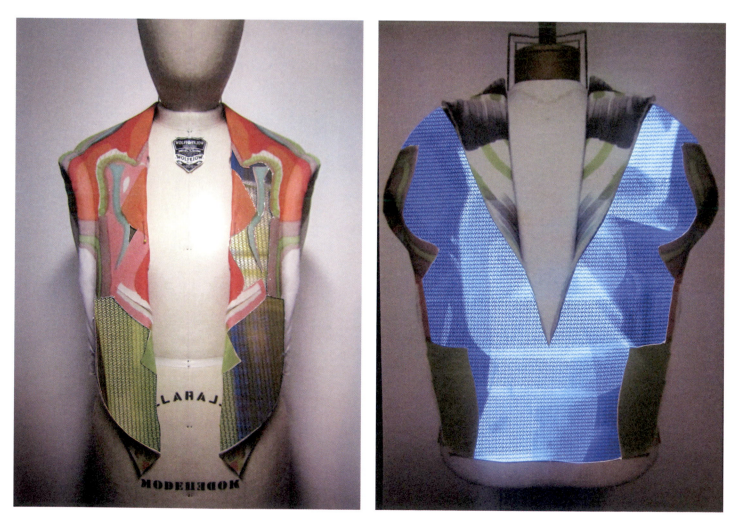

Avoid reiterating existing concepts or directly translating from your source

Leah didn't have to be concerned about direct translation of the source material, because she created it. Everything she chose to use from her research ended up in an original translation because she created her own visuals as a result. By creating some original artwork, she gave the rest of the project a very personal aesthetic and direction.

3 / 4 / 5 / 6
Light-up garments
Leah used EL paper over a layer of foam to incorporate and light up the graphics of the photographs on her fabric.

5

6

Turn to page 56 to see PART I (Idea) of this project, or page 184 for PART III (Design).

Soft, draped silhouettes, suspended away from the physical body.

Process

Visual research	**3D innovation**	2D visualization
Spirit visualization	**2D sketching**	2D / 3D draping
3D concepts	**3D draping**	3D development
Observational research	**Materiality**	2D sketch line-up
Narrative research	**3D construction**	Editorial photography
3D construction	**3D tailoring**	

'Tensegrity' by Aura Taylor

127

PART I
Idea / **Practice**
62

PART II
Concept / Practice
↓

PART III
Design / *Practice*
190

Tensegrity

Aura Taylor

On pages 62–67, we saw how Aura researched acupuncture and structural systems to start the creative process.

How, what, where, when and why?

After developing 3D 'lace' with pins and thread on the dress form, Aura started sourcing materials, doodling and sketching out her initial design ideas. Within this process she also worked with 2D/3D draping to better visualize shapes in 3D. She sourced perforated suede and leathers that would further reinforce the acupuncture idea, flocked face neoprene foam to support the 3D 'lace', along with rivets, silk and elastic cords, and coated nylon/silk organza. The fabrics were selected with two main criteria in mind: first based on her personal taste and the clean, modern aesthetic she sought, with pronounced geometry achieved in the silhouettes within the collection; and second the stiffness and/or thickness of materials required to achieve the shapes that would extend away from the body and hold the 3D 'lace' in place.

Initially, Aura started to work from the acupuncture concept, aiming to develop a structure that would hold the 'body' of a garment. She enjoyed the effect of threads being suspended at different heights and levels and the fact that they were extending away from the body, along with the geometry and sharp linear composition they created. Her next objective was to extend these 'bio-laces' into the garments.

All of Aura's attempts to do this only led to more problems. The 3D 'lace' that she created with the pins required a solid base in order for the threads to be held in position with the right amount of tension. The fact that the pins needed to be held firmly in place in order for them to be raised at different levels without any movement was the main obstacle. While it worked on the dress form, it wouldn't work on the actual body.

Aura wanted to create something more wearable and functional and the option of using a very stiff material to hold pins in place seemed forced and unnatural, and more like building a garment to support this structure rather than the other way round. She was also hoping to use the metal pieces directly on the body and wasn't satisfied with the idea of using a stiff fabric as a base, so she started looking for a new solution to replace the pin.

This example serves as a good reminder not to get discouraged within the design process when things don't work out. Designers are problem solvers, and in most cases the best ideas come from a point of discovery. What at first seems like a failure often leads to innovation and a new solution.

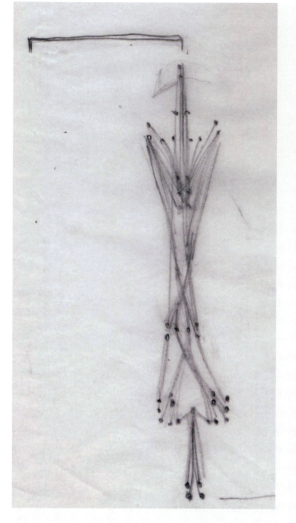

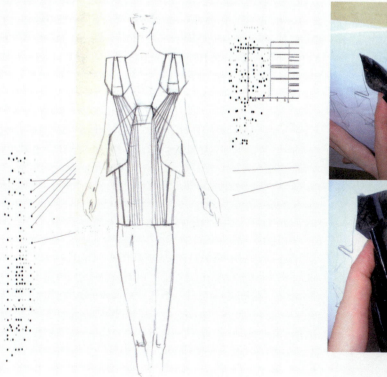

1

Ｆｉｒｓｔ ｓｋｅｔｃｈｅｓ
After experimenting with pins
and thread on the dress form, Aura
started doodling, sketching and
sourcing materials.

2

Ａｃｕｐｕｎｃｔｕｒｅ ｓｔｒｕｃｔｕｒｅｓ
Initially, Aura wanted to work with
the acupuncture concept, developing
a structure that would hold the 'body'
of the garment. She searched for
alternatives to pins that could be used
on the body.

Don't discard anything!

After researching the tensegrity principle further, Aura came across some steel constructions that inspired her to create the visual look she sought to achieve: that of a fabric being suspended in tension while allowing it to be extended away from the body. With this in mind, she began creating 3D models of a strut construction, created with hollow metal tubes and wires.

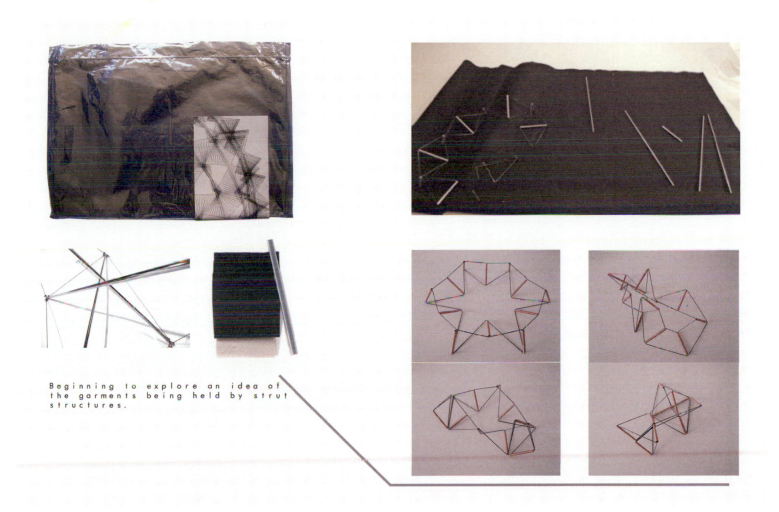

Beginning to explore an idea of the garments being held by strut structures.

3
Strut model construction, created with hollow metal tubes and wires
After investigating her 'tensegrity' theme further, Aura attempted to create a construction that would allow fabric to be suspended in tension away from the body.

Tensegrity Structure

4
Draping with jersey
Aura selected fine rayon and jersey as their elastic properties made them ideal materials. They gave a much softer aesthetic than Aura was looking for though.

5
Tailoring
Aura moved away from the softer materials to a 3D tailoring process, introducing sharper lines and silhouettes. She continued with her theme of creating clothes that were built away from the body.

Allow your own unique perspective and creative vision to guide your process

Aura positioned the strut structure on a dress form and started stretching fabric across the body, going from one structure to another and back again. She moved the structure points around various points on the body, such as the shoulder, waist and back in order to create new silhouettes. Her main goal was keeping the fabric extended away from the body. While looking to maintain the 'fabric in tension' effect, Aura narrowed down the options to the use of fine rayon and jersey. Their elastic properties and ability to stretch and create drape simultaneously made them ideal materials.

The results of the 3D draping in jersey, however, were much softer and more fluid than Aura's design aesthetic, so she went back to the 3D tailoring process to introduce sharper lines and silhouettes to balance out the softer silhouettes. She used the same concept and idea of garments that were to be built away from the body. This time she used seams to create the visual language of a mathematical blueprint of the body.

Avoid reiterating existing concepts or directly translating from your source

Aura's entire process is authentic. She utilized her research at various points to move it forward. Whether it was the geometric shapes that fed her initial exploration of the acupuncture points on the body, or her investigation into the work of Buckminster Fuller and the concept of tensegrity that took her in a new direction, she sought ways to make this process her own and solutions that would lead her down new pathways. From her personal perspective as a designer, she reimagined the tensegrity concept within the context of fashion, and as a result brought together the previously seeming opposites of biology and fashion design.

This is a wonderful example of persevering when a project seemingly comes to a dead end. Designers quickly bore of unresolved ideas, discarding them in search of 'the next thing'. But good ideas lie dormant within every project and some just need time to be fully realized within the right context. We can make connections via a new means of discovery.

5

Turn to page 62 to see PART I (Idea) of this project, or page 190 for PART III (Design).

An investigation into shape-memory materials and new craft technologies and textiles.

Process

Investigation of craft	**Fusion weaving**	Organic engineering
Data collection	**Fibre experimentation**	Natural programming
Material / scientific research	**Craft**	
Journaling	**Tradition and technology**	
Material / scientific experimentation	**Embroidery**	
Visual research	**Natural / artificial technology**	
2D sketching		

Techno Naturology

Elaine Ng Yan Ling

On pages 68–73, we saw how Elaine carried out scientific experimentation into artificial shape memory materials and natural wood substances, in a quest to find new textile technologies.

How, what, where, when and why?

After collecting all her data, Elaine had to analyse the results of the experiments. Looking back into the logbooks and revisiting the videos, she explored the hand quality of the fabric and did some durability tests through washing and heating processes.

As part of her coursework, Elaine participated in weekly critiques with and presentations to experts from the Textiles Futures Research Group, and Textiles Futures Designers. This enabled her to repeatedly question and improve the project.

In order to achieve a non-biased result, Elaine exhibited in a 'Work in Progress' exhibition, held in Central Saint Martins College of Art and Design. The exhibition showcased research projects to the general public. Pieces included some 'work-in-progress' samples of prototypes in small scale, and an animation video to demonstrate the movement concept. Visitors to the show included the general public, some of whom had good knowledge of design, fashion and technology, and others with good knowledge of architecture, mechanical and material engineering. They gave some very useful feedback, and asked pertinent questions about the functionality of Elaine's new hybrid shape-memory material.

Most of these questions centred on the issue of how much shape-memory material and how much natural material made up the hybrid. But the visitors also wanted to know whether the design worked for fashion or architecture, and how controllable the design was. Also importantly, they wanted to know whether the design concept could feasibly enter the marketplace within the next ten years.

With all these questions in mind, Elaine focused on the areas that she had not yet explored properly. Could the shape-memory polymer be used in a large scale and how could it be applied as an exterior structure? Traditionally, it would only be used on a much smaller scale, often in relation to body form. In these instances, it can be more precisely monitored and often the movement is more pronounced. Elaine's vision was to create a form that was more organic, so she wanted to investigate how it would behave on a larger scale.

Don't discard anything!

After the 'Work In Progress' exhibition, Elaine decided to look further into the issue of how much shape-memory material and how much wood veneer to include in the hybrid. This was key to the 'naturology' design. She created scenarios of what and how things could be changed and eventually found what she felt to be a good balance of the two materials.

Next, Elaine decided to revisit the traditional technique of weaving, and researched a wide range of ordinary fibres that had 'reactive' properties. These included cane, SPMV with various twisted polyester-based fibre, balsa wood, silk, monofilament and wool elastic as well as smart fibres and shape-memory fibres. These fibres can all be considered thermo-reactive as well as hydro-reactive. Investigating the individual property of these fibres allowed Elaine to carefully integrate them in the correct proportion and control the reactivity of the woven fabric.

In order to push the boundaries of traditional weaving, Elaine integrated laser-cutting technology and laminated surfaces (without involving adhesive) in her weaving process. This stage of experimentation was focused on exploring the combination of techniques and getting the proportion correct. Elaine began to layer techniques; for example, after weaving her samples and thermo-setting the shape, she would then test out new shapes by combining laser-cutting with hand carving.

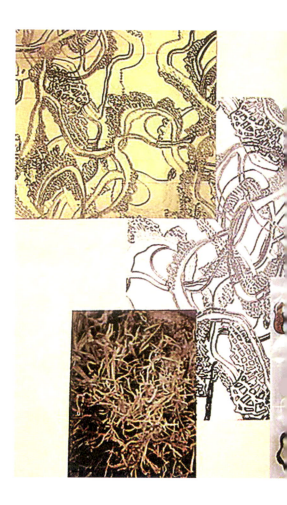

2

1

Sketchbook pages
Testing out a motif design on various materials, including wood and shape-memory polymers.

2

Work in progress exhibition
Elaine produced an exhibition to showcase early stage materialization in small prototypes and animations.

3

Fibre experimentation
Elaine combined cane, shape-memory fibre and SPMV to create a shape that is semi-predetermined by the woven structures within it.

1

From my point of view, fashion is not merely restricted within the context of clothing. Fashion is also shelter.

Elaine Ng Yan Ling

3

4

5

4 / 5

Prototyping

Elaine experimented with wood
veneer to investigate movement and
flexibility.

6

Multi-dimensionality study

Here, Elaine creates negative forms
through changes in temperature.

Allow your own unique perspective and creative vision to guide your process

Elaine now wanted to translate the findings of her research into useful data to create the 'naturology' structure. She was now ready to apply all that she had learned to both fashion and architecture.

Her challenge now was to discover how to utilize shape memory materials and allow them to make safe and comfortable contact with skin. Would it be necessary to use electrical power as a driving force or would the power of nature be enough to allow and drive movement?

This is the biggest challenge facing new technology in textiles within the fashion arena. The use of electronics within clothing is prohibitive to the wearer and Elaine needed to find a solution that would allow her to apply her concept to the real world.

She used prototyping to investigate the following areas:

— Exploring flexibility, using plastic with super
— elastic behaviours in order in obtain movement
— without extra energy being involved.

— Understanding the strengths and weaknesses of the
— shape memory polymer and alloy.

— Using natural materials such as cane, and analysing their sensitivity to changes in humidity and
— temperature).

Elaine revisited her computer programming techniques with the Arduino platform. Arduino is an open-source electronics prototyping platform based on flexible, easy-to-use hardware and software. It is intended for artists and designers interested in creating interactive objects or environments. She tested out which script would allow the movement to perform best. All these experiments were recorded via photography and video. This allowed Elaine to replay and analyse the process with her peer group. Within electronics there is always an unknown element. If there is a miscalculation, it might cause a short circuit but it might not appear at first. Hence the video record is crucial to testing.

Avoid reiterating existing concepts or directly translating from your source

Elaine coined new terms to describe her processes thus far: 'Craftnology' and 'Fusion Weaving.'

In order to move the design concept forward, it was crucial for Elaine to select successful ideas and eliminate less successful options. The prototyping stage allowed Elaine to work out which techniques were compatible with which. For example, embroidery techniques, so popular within fashion design, were not suitable for her concept. In testing, when a current was passed through the alloy, it had become very hot and had melted the fibres sewn around it. But Elaine was keen to use these traditional techniques and experimented further by sewing the alloy with different types of fibres, such as wool, paper yarn and polyester. She found that the different fibres burned at different rates and although this technique was not appropriate to use with the alloy, it inspired Elaine to develop a new weave structure.

Elaine's focus was on creating a 'live' textile, informed by nature and intrinsically reactive to its very design. A second key component of Elaine's process is the exploration of nature and the artificial. The aim of Techno 'Naturology' was to apply natural responses to the design of engineering systems and modern technology, thereby mimicking a hybrid tectonic system.

The hybrid tectonic system is an intelligent, kinetic system, achieved by mimicking the responsive systems of both artificial and natural sensors, and used in technology to create architectural structures that address a dynamic, flexible and constantly changing demand. It enables buildings to adapt their form, shape, colour or character responsively, and can be refined and extended to improve the perception of spatial experience. Elaine uses the same system here to develop her innovative textile.

Turn to page 68 to see PART I (Idea) of this project, or page 196 for PART III (Design).

Academic Perspective
Timo Rissanen

What is your design philosophy and how does this impact your teaching?

My primary concern is for the survival of humanity in the face of an uncertain future, and therefore I provide the students with the context within which fashion design and culture exist. While systems thinking has not traditionally been a part of fashion design education, it will need to be in the future.

When designing the physical garments, I begin with two things: the human body and the cloth, and for me fashion design is about exploring the different possible relationships between the two. Returning to systems thinking, concerns about the entire garment life cycle inform my thinking, stemming from the acknowledgement that what I design is not 'finished' – the garment will continue to exist and create different impacts once it leaves my hands. I share this with my students, albeit with the recognition that their philosophies are not mine. As an educator, I believe my role is to support my students in forming their own philosophies about their place in the world as designers.

What methods do you use as an instructor to inspire students to excel beyond their limitations?

I constantly aim to open students' eyes to aspects of the world around us of which they may not currently be aware. In any given class, I remind myself several times that my role is to inspire students to find their own voice.

Can you describe any specific methodologies or frameworks you have developed in your teaching (that are unique to your approach)?

With regards to zero-waste fashion design, pattern cutting and mark making are integral to the design process. Even where fabric waste is not a concern, I have noticed that encouraging a student to begin with two-dimensional patterns (instead of two-dimensional sketches of garments) can lead to new, unexpected garment forms.

Often when I recognize that a student struggles to innovate through sketching, I encourage collage instead of sketching. For example, Laura Li, a BFA senior at Parsons, used sections of photographs of stone quarries by Edward Burtunsky to collage her 'sketches'. She then used these as guides in draping the garments in the collection.

What is the source of your approach? How did it evolve?

The source of my approach is everything I have done to date in my life, as well as through the many inspiring people I have been blessed to meet during my career in fashion. I was taught a somewhat conventional approach to design: research, sketch, pattern cut, make. In my final year, however, I had a teacher, Val Horridge, who was open to me working in half-scale to create 3D drapes. These drapes were further developed through sketching; the draping led to garment forms that I wouldn't have been able to develop otherwise.

During my PhD research into zero-waste fashion design, pattern cutting became integral to my design process. I realized early on that designing zero-waste garments solely through sketching was not possible, and that pattern cutting had to commence before the idea was finalized. Now, wasting fabric is no longer an option for me; everything I do is zero-waste. I don't experience this as a limitation, however, but as an opportunity for highly creative approaches to designing clothes.

Timo Rissanen taught fashion in Australia for seven years and has a particular interest in sustainable fashion. His design process is influenced by 'inquisitive' pattern cutting and he has carried out in-depth research into zero-waste design through his studies and practice.

When a student hits a wall in their process, how do you help them to move forward?

First, I try to recognize what is happening by listening to the student. Then I suggest a number of solutions for moving forward, and discuss these with the student. For example, a student will present somewhat ordinary (or 'known') sketches and a number of written ideas for very rich textile development but no experimentation in actual cloth. Asking the student to stop talking or writing about cloth and textile development and instead focus on 'getting their hands dirty' and experimenting with manipulating and embellishing cloth will help the student find their own language around fashion and textiles.

Do you think there is a 'right' or 'wrong' way to design?

It is difficult for me to make a judgment on different design processes in terms of 'right' or 'wrong'. Every designer has a different world view and different design methods. When teaching fashion design, however, I argue that imposing one's own approach or philosophy on a student is a questionable approach. Teachers of design in any discipline must recognize that students' learning styles are diverse, and that the design process is individual and personal. Our common goal should be the pursuit of holistic beauty. This beauty does not include slave labour or destruction of the natural environment.

Can you share your thoughts on the importance of the following:

Research: Without thorough research, there can be no innovation. Visual research, while crucial to developing a personal take on aesthetics, is not enough to develop a comprehensive design concept. A successful designer needs to be a voracious reader.

Experimentation/design development: A certain fearlessness is required. Giving up the fear of failure that is instilled in us since early childhood is important, if challenging. From mistakes, disasters and catastrophes, new ideas and unexpected learning can emerge.

Process: Create your own process. This will take some trial and error, and time. In time, you will learn what kinds of processes suit and serve you best.

Vision/aesthetics/taste: These are inseparable from research. Part of any designer's research is living a 'rich' life: being open to new experiences, and being pathologically curious about the world that surrounds us.

Identity as designer: This is key to self-expression. What do you want to say through your work?

Self-reflection: I believe self reflection is the key tool for moving the design process forward. This is not to say it is always easy. Both students and professionals get very 'close' to their work and sometimes it is difficult to have perspective and the distance required to reflect. Without critical reflection there is no learning.

What advice would you give to students or emerging designers who are still seeking to establish their identity and aesthetic?

Try to recognize what methods of designing are best suited to you as a designer and as a human being. Live and experience the world; the richer your experiences, the more you will have to draw from. At times, give up the right to be right.

If you could distil your approach into one sentence, what would that be?

Really hear the world, really see the world, really taste the world.

Designer Perspective
Maria Cornejo

What is your design philosophy?

Minimalism is a lot harder than it looks. It's easy to embellish and add things, but it's a challenge to make things appear simple but still be beautiful and flattering. I try to use basic geometric shapes as the building blocks for how I design my collections. I like to use as few seams as possible in the garments as well. Figuring out this puzzle keeps the design process interesting for me, and then seeing a simple shape transformed on the body is the creative pay-off!

How do you work? What is the first step in your design process? Is it always the same?

For me to feel inspired, I have to remove myself as far away from clothes as possible. I have to reject everything to initiate a desire and think to myself, what do I want? What do I need? Once I start to desire is when I can begin to create a collection.

How did your design process evolve? Has the process changed over time?

I'm still constantly redefining and evolving my ideas and looking for new ways to provoke and challenge myself. It's important for me to be learning and continuously challenged.

Is your process instinctual or learned, or a combination of both?

Both. But also experience has allowed me to create shortcuts.

Do you understand your process to be linear (building one design from another) or somewhat random?

The collection tends towards an evolution – building on concepts and design elements from the past. There are always the same elements in the collection – volume, draping, minimalism, but I'm pushing the collection forward by throwing in unexpected elements each season. A lot of the time, I'll be inspired to try something different or pull something from the archive five or six years back and rework it. We also repeat successful styles – clothes should be long-lasting and timeless.

This book addresses multiple entry points to design: literal, narrative, abstract, 2D visual, 2D flat pattern, 3D deconstruction, 3D construction, narrative, mind-mapping, textile innovation and new technologies. Which of these best describes your process?

My design process is mostly 2D flat pattern, 3D construction/deconstruction. I typically start from the fabrics and then continue to 3D draping.

If you could distil your approach to design into one sentence, what would that be?

The collection is named 'zero' as an expression of a pure vision: zero is a number that neither adds nor subtracts; it is, rather, a point of departure.

Maria Cornejo's varied career spans London, Paris, Milan and Tokyo, where she was part of the ground-breaking design partnership Richmond Cornejo. She then developed her own signature 'Maria Cornejo' collection and worked as a creative consultant for major retailers Joseph, Tehen and Jigsaw.

In 1996, Maria and her family moved to New York and in 1997, she transformed a raw space in Nolita into a highly creative atelier and store. Her uncompromising and very personal approach has gained her a loyal following and high praise from clients such as Tilda Swinton, Michelle Williams and Cindy Sherman. Cornejo has also custom-made pieces for the First Lady, Michelle Obama.

In May 2006, 'Zero Maria Cornejo' opened its second store in New York's Far West Village. The 'Zero + Maria Cornejo' collection is presented biannually during New York Fashion Week and in Milan and Paris. The line is sold in leading stores around the world such as Barneys New York, Holt Renfrew Toronto & Montreal, Ikram Chicago, Blake Chicago, Weathervane Santa Monica, Grocery Store San Francisco and Mac San Francisco, Dover Street Market London, Joyce Boutique Hong Kong and Villa Moda in Dubai.

When or if you hit a wall in your process, how do you move forward?

I'll leave it and come back to it later. I will either go for a walk or work on something else. I typically have to step away in order to move forward.

Do you think there is a 'right' or 'wrong' way to design?

There is no right or wrong. Only what works best for you.

What, do you find, is most important to your process?

For me, the most important starting point is my own identity as a designer and its important that I stick with it. I will experiment with shapes and abstract concepts but always making it wearable and realistic. I do a lot of self-reflection of who I am as a designer and what my designs mean. I believe that's the process. But I rarely do research.

What advice would you give to students or emerging designers who are still seeking to establish their identity and aesthetic?

Find your own voice, your own path.

Point of View

Fashion Journalist, Mickey Boardman
Paper magazine

A superlatively flaming ubiquity in New York's downtown social circles, **Mickey Boardman** is a parody of fierceness and author of the 'Ask Mr. Mickey' column for *Paper* magazine.

How do you view your role in relation to the designer?

Well I've had disagreements with other journalists about our role. I think first and foremost I'm a cheerleader for fashion. Every show I go to I want to love, I want the designer to sell tons of clothes to retailers, I want them to get tons of good press. I basically want the best for them. My role at the publication is to shine the light on undiscovered talents and try to spread the good news about them.

How should emerging designers balance their creative vision with financial stability while navigating the fashion system?

It's a tough fork in the road...balancing financial stability with creative vision. Every designer is different and you really can't compare. Young designers need to figure out who they want to be and decide if they want to create a niche market.

But we need to remember that Marc Jacobs went out of business in the early days, lost backers and had so many years of struggle. It's hard to imagine that now with his success at Dior. Then look at Michael Kors who has a giant business but also had lean years growing his business.

What impact do you think reviews have on emerging designers? Can they make or break them?

If you get covered in the key papers and have a photo, then retailers call to place the order. You need to get the right press to get into stores and you need the stores to get the press... if it's not in editorial, stores don't want to buy, and will say, 'let us know when you get coverage – we don't like to shoot something if it's not available in stores'. So it is a terrible catch twenty-two. Emerging designers think, 'I have to get press so I have to design something editorial', but the editorial pieces aren't going to sell and it all becomes a juggling act. It's not black and white.

It's important to note too that if key players in the industry support a designer, it can change their career – they're the people with the power.

What do you highlight when reviewing a new designer/collection? By categorizing their strengths do you become a key player in defining the trajectory of their career?

We aren't going to talk about whether it's wearable or reasonably priced etc. That has no bearing on whether it's good or not. We just look for someone that makes us excited.

People are shocked when they ask us for some of our favourite designers and we list Michael Kors. They think we only like junky freaks and clowns but he does beautiful, classic American sportswear – that's a point of view just the same way Duro Olowo and Isabel Toledo have their point of view. We just love fabulous clothes.

Are you looking for an articulated vision that is growing season to season?

To me, it's an insult (that some celebrated young designers are very are guilty of) when designers try to be totally different each season so you don't know who they are. One season they are Balenciaga, the next they are Givenchy. I love someone who knows who they are.

Do you view the designer's process as key in developing their vision, aesthetic and point of view as a designer? This may not be apparent to the customer but when you meet with designers do you have a sense of that?

I don't know too much about their process. I guess it comes down to whatever works for the designer. For example, Anna Sui's last show was the best she had ever done. When I interviewed her backstage, she was so happy. If it's great then it shows through.

What makes a collection successful, from your point of view?

For me it has nothing to do with saleability or wearability – it's about being amazing. I think about collections I love that changed by life: the Comme des Garçons clown collection with knits, giant polka dots, cotton-candy wigs on the runway. To me, a collection is successful if it makes an impact on anyone – whether it's customers, press, editors, retailers, anyone… and if it changes the direction of fashion.

What's more important? Commercial viability, creativity or a marriage of both?

It's a weird balancing act. When I was younger I would have said it was all about creativity. But creativity doesn't pay the bills. The goal is to be as creative as possible while being financially viable… it's about the balance.

How do you assess raw talent?

It's a funny thing about young talent. I'm a photo editor so I see a lot of photographers. I'll ask them to bring in their work and some will say, 'I'm not ready! I'm not ready!' They think they need to get a super fancy portfolio, with their name embossed in a wooden box. I remember one of the best photographers that came to see me – she came in with a box – just a box. She was so clueless on a certain level, and the opposite extreme of the others I described, but she was a genius printer. She showed me photos of roadkill. Now I'm a vegetarian and don't eat meat so to bring me photos of roadkill wasn't such a great idea! But she had such a unique point of view and her work made such an impression on me that I said, 'Let's do something together.' Designers are the same way. You have to do a show or a presentation of some kind. It doesn't take renting the Grand Palais. Just do good work.

Anything that shows the personality and uniqueness of the work is successful. But if you are doing it just to get attention then that's not good either. It's very nuanced. When it's different and good it's fabulous but when it's different and bad it's not!

What advice would you give to a fashion design graduate?

Be yourself. If I say I love Rick Owens it's because he is so unique – you see his clothing and know what it is – it doesn't mean he is rich but he is doing his thing.

FASHI
THI
PART III

Desy

'The best way to predict the future is to design it.'
Buckminster Fuller

gn

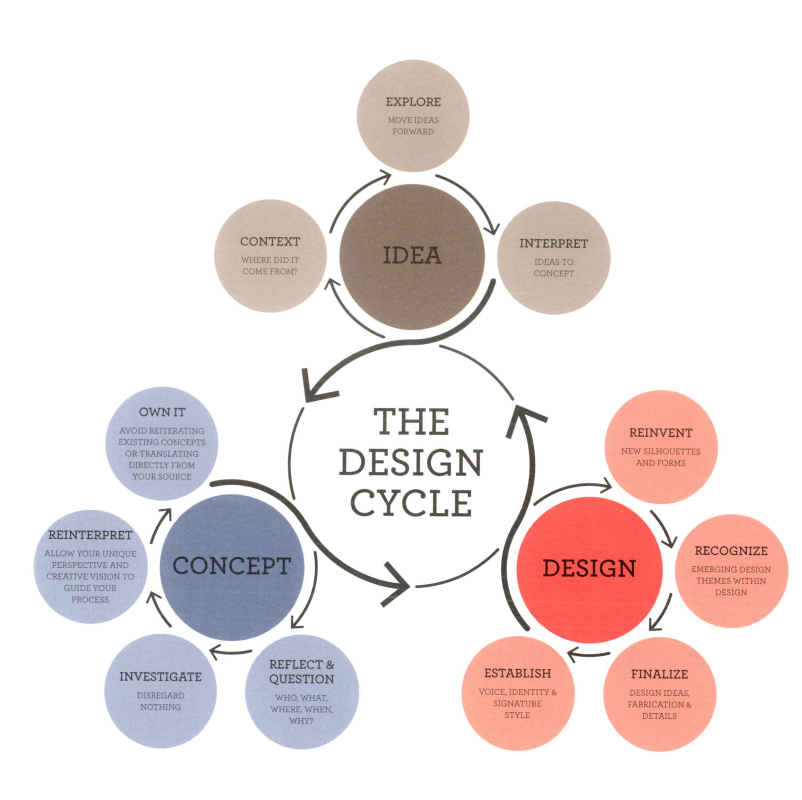

THE DESIGN CYCLE

EXPLORE
MOVE IDEAS FORWARD

IDEA

CONTEXT
WHERE DID IT COME FROM?

INTERPRET
IDEAS TO CONCEPT

OWN IT
AVOID REITERATING EXISTING CONCEPTS OR TRANSLATING DIRECTLY FROM YOUR SOURCE

REINTERPRET
ALLOW YOUR UNIQUE PERSPECTIVE AND CREATIVE VISION TO GUIDE YOUR PROCESS

CONCEPT

INVESTIGATE
DISREGARD NOTHING

REFLECT & QUESTION
WHO, WHAT, WHERE, WHEN, WHY?

REINVENT
NEW SILHOUETTES AND FORMS

DESIGN

RECOGNIZE
EMERGING DESIGN THEMES WITHIN DESIGN

ESTABLISH
VOICE, IDENTITY & SIGNATURE STYLE

FINALIZE
DESIGN IDEAS, FABRICATION & DETAILS

Design / Process

design:
- to create, fashion, execute, or construct according to plan
- to have as a purpose
- to devise for a specific function or end
- to indicate with a distinctive mark, sign, or name
- to conceive or execute a plan
- to draw, lay out, or prepare a design

This final stage of design is the culmination of the work done in the previous two phases. Prior research and exploration are synthesized into a fully realized collection. Authenticity is paramount and it is critical for designers to remain open to new ideas, even at this stage. Radical new departures often occur as 2D ideas take shape in three-dimensional form. Epiphanies arise that might require starting over, which is better than risking mediocrity or a disjointed collection.

Editing is a critical part of this stage in the process. Students sometimes short-circuit themselves by self-editing too early at the ideation stage, often stripping away the innovative ideas that are the very essence of their authenticity as a designer. Merchandising is important to an extent (and for some this is a viable working method and approach to design throughout the entire process), but many end up compromising their designs by embracing this practice too soon and abdicating their desire to express a vision beyond what is considered 'commercially' viable. In this instance, if they don't attempt to express their vision they will end up with a diluted version of their original concepts and familiar – but not innovative – silhouettes. Originality in design is not merely changing a fabric, a colour or tweaking a lapel shape; it is much more than this.

In the final process of refining gold, the impurities are burnt off. Similarly, in the final stages of design, the designer hones their ideas until the very last second aiming to reach perfection and communicating the vision into a tangible reality. Even as the model is waiting to exit, the designer is tweaking, making final edits and finessing the look for final impact.

During this final phase where ideas and concepts coalesce, you should seek to articulate your own visual language and personal design vocabulary. Your personal way of working automatically reflects this and your design identity emerges over time as you begin to recognize your own strengths and particular approach to design.

For Isabel Toledo, the overarching approach to her work can be described in what she calls 'dressing emotion'. Her exploratory process became her language. She says, 'I had taught myself to drape in motion. I recall the freeing feeling, like removing the training wheels of a bike, as I worked out shapes that resembled three-dimensional versions of the flat paper patterns I had first loved when I started sewing. All of this playing around would one day become my language and my complete body of work, I was learning how to communicate emotions visually, because I was always trying to design clothes that captured a feeling.' (Isabel Toledo, 2012, *Roots of Style: Weaving Together Life, Love and Fashion*)

An investigation into movement and dance, using zero waste and sustainable methods.

Process

Brainstorming / free association

Mind mapping

Music / Dance

Video

2D painting

Photography

Doodling

Surface print design

Textile / knit development

Zero-waste flat pattern

2D sketching

3D draping

Surface textile design

Self-editing

Recycling

3D draping and construction

Fabric manipulation

Zero-waste cutting

Textile innovation

Ethics

Sustainable practice

Hope for the Future

Janelle Abbott

On pages 84–89, we saw how Janelle further developed her ideas through a process of self-editing, to create abstract silhouettes that inferred her concept of motion.

Reinvent new silhouettes and forms

Janelle's final concept, inspired by dance, was one that literally threw the garments away from the body. The silhouettes were whirling dervishes suspended in space and time, with garments twisting around the body, restricting it in some places, and letting it loose in others. In particular, the oversized garments Janelle wore in the performance pieces informed many of the silhouettes. For example, a full circle skirt revealed its entire circle, an oversized men's shirt revealed sagging sleeves, creating a distorted body. The forms were sloppy and oversized, sitting heavily on top, spinning around or falling off the body.

Janelle thought she had developed a technique that would uniquely illustrate the idea of 'capturing motion', until she took a trip with a friend to a department store and found out that someone had already explored this very theme. But she pushed forward nonetheless. She took a swatch of power-mesh fabric and a much larger swatch of muslin, and stretched the power-mesh to the edges of the muslin, sewing around the swatch so that the larger piece of fabric underneath appeared wrinkled and trapped through the webbing of the power-mesh. She found that this technique was a good way to illustrate some of the untamable motion produced through the act of dance, but also, it referenced the hand of the artist in her attempts to grasp and hold onto motion before it found its chance to slip away. This technique, then, brought the fabric close to the body, but did little to let the material loose. Keeping this in mind, she only used this technique on portions of the garments.

The silhouettes were highly dependent on the weight and quality of materials; some fabrics were both heavy and stiff, and others were soft and loose. With the latter, Janelle employed substances such as thick layers of house paint in certain areas to contain or create the shape of the garment. For example, on a dress where the body wrapped around the torso but the skirt flew away in a spiral motion, she painted over the rippling fabric of the torso, but was more sparing on the skirt. This allowed shape to be kept on the torso, but also allowed the wearer of the garment to see and feel a certain level of paused motion. In addition, the wearer was also able to imbue their own motion into the garment.

Recognize emerging themes within design

The overarching theme emerged as simple and singular: garments caught in moments of motion. As it manifested, it determined the forms and silhouettes and when decorated, it referenced a whirlwind of influences encountered through this particular process of design.

The mind mapping processes in particular had helped Janelle to solidify her aspirations to design through a multimedia process. By openly accepting the pursuit of parallel arts, she had opened up a channel for considering the conceptualization and creation of a garment from ulterior initiation points: movement, music, glimpses, and passing thoughts.

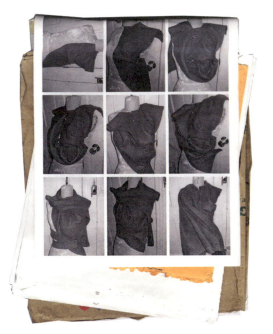

1 / 2

Developing shape and silhouette

Central to Janelle's concept was the theme of garments caught in moments of motion. A number of techniques including drawing and 3D draping, helped to capture this in the designs.

3

Surface techniques

Janelle also used the initial brush stroke patterns that had emerged from her reactions to the music to inform the surface design of her garments.

4

Final looks

Janelle felt that the idea of motion was constantly propelling her collection forward.

Finalize design ideas, fabrication and details

Janelle describes her final theme as 'a capsule of space restricted to a particular moment in time. The pieces fight, fuse, and find themselves unified inside.'

She paid careful consideration to the construction of each garment; she wanted each piece to be created through the zero-waste cutting technique (where every square inch of fabric is used in the production of a garment, thus producing no waste). Applied to her process, this meant that Janelle frequently had to approach a garment idea backwards. She would begin by designing a pattern where the pieces could fit together like a puzzle, before being cut out and assembled to form a garment.

Hand-painted elements, embroidery, abstracted prints coupled with obtrusive prints, hand-knits, and rainbow gradients were also common themes in Janelle's work. The initial brush strokes were evident in the embroidered patterns scattered across many of the pieces.

The garment shapes were developed directly from the stills taken during the dance portion of the project. Textiles were chosen and manipulated in a specific manner in order to ensure that though stationary, the illusion of motion would be maintained.

The knits also helped to express the concept of 'moments of motion'. By catching stitches long after they had been knitted, Janelle ripped and piled the garments upon themselves, again capturing this idea of motion. She also stumbled across a new technique thanks to a dyeing accident. As she had been developing this process, she used a colour of cotton yarn that she was later unhappy with. To remove the colour, she used a special dye remover solution, but rather than having the desired effect, it turned the latter portion of the knit swatch blue. The ombré effect that this generated was actually something that Janelle liked, and was recreated by a swatch of rainbow watercolour in the final collection.

5

6

7

Establish your voice, identity and signature style

Janelle's personal convictions inform her work ethic and her design philosophy. She was keen to create something entirely alone, without requiring additional wasteful labour and resources.

Janelle was also keen to establish the link between her final collection and the song that had initially given rise to it: 'In listening to the words and the many musical changes that this 17-minute song goes through, I felt urged to consider what kinds of hopes I had for the future. I wanted the collection to reflect my hopefulness that the quality of my life (emotional and mental) would become increasingly more stable, and peaceful, as the future progressed. But also, I hoped the same for others. That when they viewed and experienced this collection, they would become in tune with the hope that I laced throughout the conceptualized pieces.'

5 / 6 / 7 / 8

Paint, dye and embroidery samples
Janelle used a number of techniques, including hand-painting, embroidery, hand knitting and rainbow gradients in her final collection.

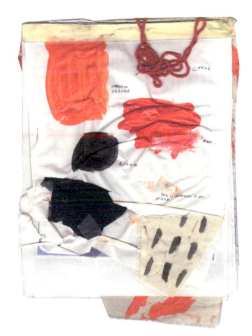

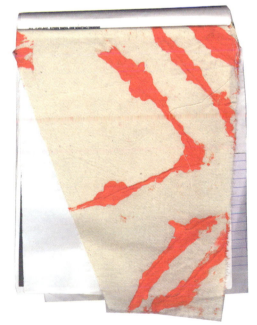

8

Turn to page 20 to see PART I (Idea) of this project, or page 84 for PART II (Concept).

A collection based on culture and social processes, from garment design to presentation.

Process

Observational research	2D visualization	**3D construction**
Narrative	Fashion cultural reference	**Brainstorming**
Digital technology	3D deconstruction	**2D / 3D visualization**
Brainstorming	2D collage	**Digital technical flat drawing**
2D sketching	Narrative	
Journaling	3D draping	**2D editing**
Digital collage	Colour / fabrication	**Exhibition**
Exhibition	2D flat pattern	

Virtual Appropriation
Melitta Baumeister

On pages 90–95, we saw how Melitta further developed her concept by deconstructing a men's suit both digitally and on the dress form, to create new silhouettes.

Reinvent new silhouettes and forms

The first two garments that Melitta constructed were derived from one jacket shape. The second piece was a bodysuit that had padding in the shape of the first jacket. The third and fourth outfits 'copied' each other in that the fourth used a jacket-shaped flock print on a transparent organza dress and the third used a shirt-shaped flock print on a transparent organza dress.

By questioning processes in society, I want to reflect social issues within fashion, giving meaning to my work. Melitta Baumeister

Recognize emerging themes within design

The emerging theme running through Melitta's work was the creation of a concept that goes beyond the garment. For her, it was key that the project was further developed through its presentation – her design was not just about the garments, but also about how they are presented within their meaning and context.

Melitta had a consistent approach to design and followed certain steps within her process throughout her projects. Firstly, she observed reality, society and things going on around her. She was constantly questioning and creating the concept in order to drive her ideas forward. This helped her to understand what she was observing or seeing. She developed this further via brainstorming and finding keywords that inspired her and related to the original concept. From keywords, she gathered ideas for details and techniques for fabric manipulation.

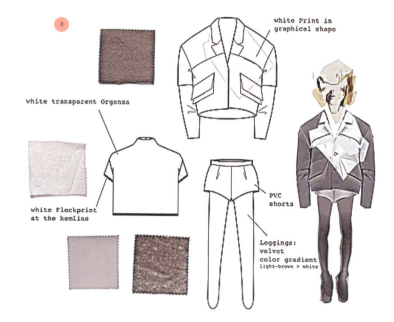

Finalize design ideas, fabrication and details

In this final stage, Melitta began to define her designs and redrew each outfit as a technical drawing using Adobe Illustrator software. She had to make final decisions within the line-up of the collection. Since it contained mostly jackets, or tops and dresses similar to the shape of a jacket, the balance of colour and silhouette was key to driving this process forward. She chose longer trousers and used tights in those looks within the line-up where the colour needed to be darker (since the colour of legs would make the single outfit lighter). The outfits with darker colours show less body/legs in the bottom components, while the lighter colour outfits reveal more of the leg, have tights in skin colour or white transparent skirts or shorts.

Key components of the collection included: graphic, polygonal shapes; a colour palette representing an equable transition from light, soft pastel colours to heavy, strong and dark colours; and fabrics and different detailed techniques to be repeated in different garments.

Melitta arranged a line-up of her entire collection and the final presentation of her collection was presented in the 'shop' she simulated. For the daytime she used real models instead of mannequins and at night the clothes were hanging on the rail.

In Pforzheim, the small city where she lived, any change was noticed. Melitta found this concept intriguing so she conducted an experiment and wrote 'Prada' on the shop window. Everybody who lived there knew it could not be true as this large luxury brand would never open a store in this small city, therefore it must be a simulation.

Melitta communicated the premise of the project to the general public by replacing the typical 'enter' sign on the door with an explanation of the concept of the work. So rather than entering the shop, the visitor would be 'entering' the idea itself.

Residents were surprised as they walked by the window and questioned what they saw. This response was exactly what Melitta had been hoping for; she wanted to challenge truth and the perception of a shop window as a metaphor for a virtual window of what is presented as reality. The brand name of Prada was used only as a metaphor as a component of the exhibition.

1 / 2 / 3 / 4

Computer collages
Melitta used digital tools to copy and paste parts of designs and to visualize looks, ideas and colours for her collection.

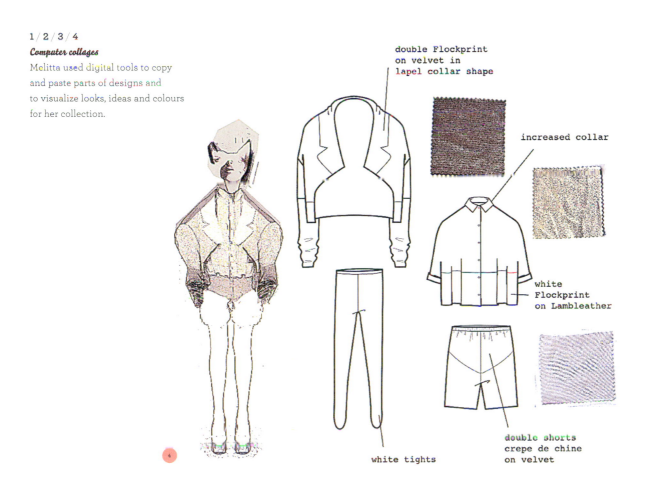

double Flockprint on velvet in lapel collar shape

increased collar

white Flockprint on Lambleather

double shorts crepe de chine on velvet

white tights

5

Final line-up

Melitta's final collection was made up
of graphic, polygonal shapes and a
combination of strong and dark and
soft, pastel colours.

Establish your voice, identity and signature style

Melitta approached her design process from a conceptual standpoint. She tried to reach a wide horizon within her concepts: 'By questioning processes in society, I want to reflect/mediate social issues within fashion, giving meaning to my work. The reflection of society with fashion is how I work and is an important step, since I see fashion always as a reaction to culture and social processes.'

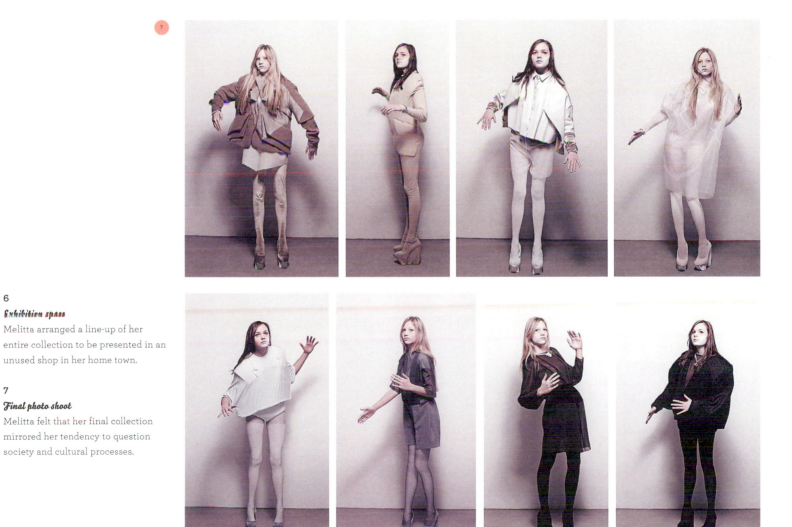

6

Exhibition space

Melitta arranged a line-up of her entire collection to be presented in an unused shop in her home town.

7

Final photo shoot

Melitta felt that her final collection mirrored her tendency to question society and cultural processes.

Turn to page 26 to see **PART I (Idea)** of this project, or page 90 for **PART II (Concept)**.

Textile innovation driven by an investigation into what lies beneath the skin.

Process

2D visualization	2D visualization	**Self-reflection**
Narrative	3D draping	**Textile innovation**
Textile exploration	2D flat pattern	**3D draping**
Hand craft	Printing technology	**Sustainable practice**
Embroidery	Textile surface design	**Technology**
Knitting		**Collaboration**
Digital technology		**Hand craft**
		Editorial photography

Neurovision
Jovana Mirabile

On pages 96–101, we saw how Jovana investigated the concept of a muse and experimented with new technologies to create head-to-toe looks in a variety of colours, textures and patterns.

Reinvent new silhouettes and forms

With a clear vision of what was to be achieved in terms of silhouette, this stage entered into a linear process. Jovana draped on the dress form with the final fabric, seeking to capture the idea of prints, pattern and texture enveloping the body. (This approach is atypical to the usual process where one works in calico or muslin to avoid mistakes.) No pattern cutting was involved at this stage. Using sketches and photos of 3D concepts as guides for overall shape, this organic process was open to change as the fabric dictated the direction of the silhouette.

1
Draping the knit on the body
Unusually, Jovana decided to drape on the dress form with the final fabric.

Recognize emerging themes within design

Recognizing good design in one's own work can be difficult. Often, it is best to seek the assessment of others whom you trust – those who can objectively point to strong ideas. Ask questions and seek to understand why one idea works and another does not. Don't just plough through your process without stopping to understand and evaluate it.

The design process itself dictates emergent themes. This is again an opportunity to reflect and assess the process to date and to recognize existing design themes. This represents a secondary stage of self-reflection. Where the process has been linear, themes become extremely apparent and where the process is more random, they are less evident and need more thought to define. In Jovana's case the message had been consistent throughout, with textile innovation leading the way in the design development phase and 3D draping being integral to the entire process. The collection is full of soft, structured shapes, underscored by intense colour blocking and a collision of prints, colour and texture.

Sustainability is a growing consideration for the design community; it is no longer a trend but a lifestyle to be embraced. For Jovana, this was central to her work in the final stages of her process. The minimization of waste became an integral part of the garment construction throughout the collection. Wherever possible, side seams were eliminated, from panelled leggings to gowns. AirDye® technology (a dyeing process that requires no water) eliminated the need for linings by printing double-faced solid/print fabrics and allowing reversibility to maximize options in several garments.

The influence of technology was also present throughout the three stages of the process and this was most evident in this final phase, where Jovana experimented with the use of fluorescent glow-in-the-dark thread, using it as embroidered embellishment. This technique was utilized in the final photo shoot, realizing the initial ideas of muse. Here we see the actualization of Jovana's concept fleshed out, with her particular vision and perspective brought to life.

3

2

Finalize design ideas, fabrication and details

At this stage coordinating accessories was key to accentuating the vision of this particular collection and allowed for further stylization. Jovana was selected as one of eight students sponsored by The Shoe Polytechnic in Padova, Italy. As a result, two shoe designs were produced in three different colourways, with print designs used as sock linings. In addition, Jovana hand-crafted coordinating bags using bright leather, printed fabrics, hand embellishment and Swarovski crystals. The crystals were also used to create original jewellery designs to complete the final vision. Here we see collaboration again providing opportunities to enhance the designer's vision.

Since textile development was so intrinsic to the evolution of this collection, the decisions to finalize fabrics were made from the onset. AirDye® prints formed the core of the collection along with cashmere wool and a knit jacquard. Additional sponsorship from Swarovski Crystal Elements™ allowed for hand-embroidery techniques to further embellish key silhouettes and necklines, emphasizing this technique in accents of piping along with fluorescent threadwork.

2
AirDye®-printed reversible jacket and Sarina dress
AirDye® technology allowed the garments to be reversible and helped to cut down on waste.

3
Chunky hand-knit glowing in backlight
The final phase of Jovana's process saw an increase in the effects of new technologies. Here, she has used a glow-in-the-dark thread as an embroidered embellishment.

4 / 5
Zania bag and Analisa shoe, AirDye®-printed clutch
Coordinating accessories were key to the vision of Jovana's collection.

6 / 7 / 8
*Embroidery sample development and
Swarovski embellishment (detail)*
Hand embroidery techniques
enhanced Jovana's collection.

9
The fully realized muse
Jovana's passion for bold, bright
colours and a mix of print and texture
gave her collection a youthful,
contemporary edge.

Establish your voice, identity and signature style

Emerging designers often struggle to identify their aesthetic. The best way to achieve this is to assess your strengths – don't try to be all things to all people. Sometimes a designer will short-circuit success by trying to emulate another person's design aesthetic. This never works. You need to find your own voice. Be true to yourself, recognize who you are and listen for consistency within the feedback you receive.

Good design represents the spirit of the designer; it has authenticity that cannot be replicated. Jovana's passion and affinity for working with colour, textile and textures is evident in her style and aesthetic. For her it's always a case of more is more! Bold, bright colours and a heavy mix of prints, textures and embellishments are mainstays in her design process, producing a youthful, contemporary attitude and customer.

Turn to page 32 to see PART I (Idea) of this project, or page 96 for PART II (Concept).

A reinvention of traditional craft techniques to create new textiles and garments.

Process

Research	Textile development	**'Knitted' textile development**
2D visualization	Digital technology	**Materiality**
Fabric manipulation	3D development	**3D draping**
Craft techniques	Craft technique	**Photography**
Textile research	3D form	**Editorial direction**
Materiality	2D visualization	**2D visual narration**
3D digital draping	Materiality	**Film**
Photography	Textile innovation	
Technical drawing	3D textile / draping	
3D draping		

'Knitting and Pleating' by Jie Li

167

PART I
Idea / Practice
38

PART II
Concept/Practice
102

PART III
Design / Practice
↓

Knitting and Pleating
Jie Li

On pages 102–107, we saw how Jie further developed her craft techniques to create new garments on the dress form.

Reinvent new silhouettes and forms

Jie prefers to work on the form, developing silhouettes as she goes. In this case, she chose the knitted samples she liked best and draped these on the dress form or model. In the final stage, Jie used batting to create more volume and taught herself to knit via a YouTube video. She used gigantic needles to create a three-dimensional look.

At this stage, she did more fabric testing with chiffon, organza and cotton, each time placing these strips on the dress form or working directly on the model to decide which technique she was going to use. The final 'fabric' she created comprised of multiple pleats stacked together. The type and thickness of the fabric drove the number of pleats: cotton had three pleats, organza four and chiffon five. All three were then fused together.

Due to the volume of pleating, Jie had to work with her hands to pull the strips through in some cases. She tested the fabrics to see which ones would turn and then cut some of the pleats out to make it easier where necessary.

Jie developed one silhouette and then, based on this, generated more ideas for the next one. She moved forward in this linear way, working in variations and allowing one to inform the development of the other. She focused on placement within the proportion of the body.

1

Draping and making on the dress form
Jie continued testing fabrics such as chiffon, organza and cotton, directly onto the dress form or model.

1

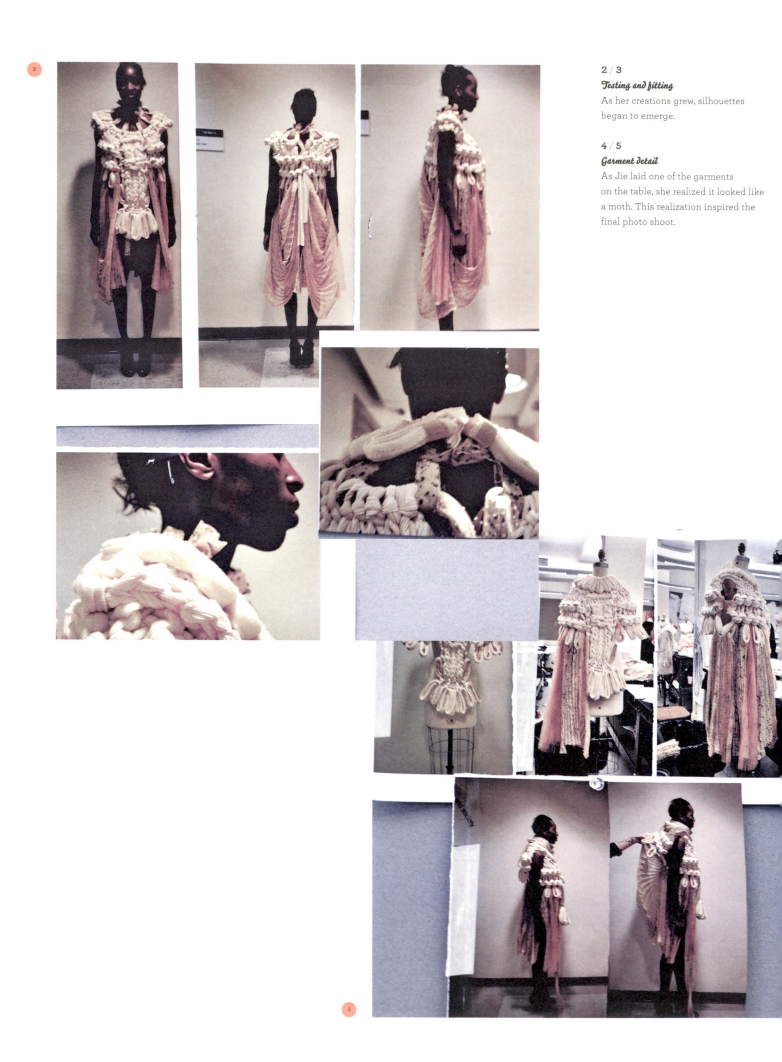

2 / 3
Testing and fitting
As her creations grew, silhouettes began to emerge.

4 / 5
Garment detail
As Jie laid one of the garments on the table, she realized it looked like a moth. This realization inspired the final photo shoot.

Recognize emerging themes within design

Handcraft techniques are foundational to the way Jie approaches design, so this project was a perfect challenge for her. Jie works in 3D and, for her, the evolution of design occurs within the process of making. She doesn't come up with concrete concepts that drive her design process forward, but merely comes across something she finds interesting (for instance the image by Lydia Hirte, which triggers an idea that she develops and makes her own).

Finalize design ideas, fabrication and details

Foundational to Jie's project was the creation of a new textile itself and this formed the basis of her approach throughout the design process. It also drove her design development and established the silhouette.

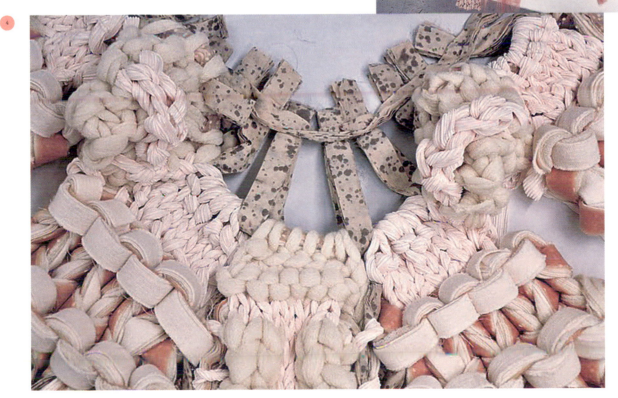

Establish your voice, identity and signature style

Within her process Jie's approach to handcrafts, fabric manipulation, relationship to technique and 3D draping is a key component in her specific approach to design. But in the final stage of the process, as Jie undertook the photo shoot, another key identity started to surface.

As Jie laid one of the garments on a table, she realized it looked like a moth. Later, during the photo shoot, the model was posing with an angry expression on her face. Jie realized she needed direction and remembered the image of the moth. This led her to create a narrative to inspire the model. 'I told her to imagine she was a moth, with broken wings. She was trying hard to fly, just like a butterfly, but sometimes she was trying so hard, it would make her angry.' Jie told the photographer to create flashes reminiscent of thunder and they set up a huge fan to create wind. Jie continued to direct the model, creating a series of vignettes that then led to the creation of a short editorial film of the model standing in one place attempting to fly.

This final approach is distinct and illustrates the spontaneity of ideas; when they arise, how they are appropriated and utilized to create visual effects. Jie made connections between a mundane moment (the way the garment lay on the table) that created a visual idea, which she then brought into the photo shoot and used for direction. The result is a poetic visual narrative of a concept that didn't exist until the final moment.

A film of Jie's work can be seen at: <www.vimeo.com/28635269>.

6 / 7

Final photo shoot

In reaction to how one of the garments had looked when laid out on a table, Jie asked her model to mimic a moth. This last-minute idea proved a success!

Turn to page 38 to see PART I (Idea) of this project, or page 102 for PART II (Concept).

Functional separates, designed for longevity and adaptation.

Process

Video

2D sketching

Brainstorming

List making

Journaling

Textile development

Colour

Silhouette

Customization

Problem solving

Technical flat sketching

Visual merchandising

Designing 'piece-by-piece'

Design editing and research

Textile development

Journaling

Narrative

Self-reflection

Journaling

Final editing

2D styling

Knitwear development

Flat sketching

Fabrication

2D final presentation

PART I
Idea / **Practice**
44

PART II
Concept/Practice
108

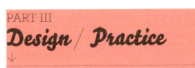

PART III
Design / *Practice*
↓

Growth and Decay

Andrea Tsao

Reinvent new silhouettes and forms

All of Andrea's work for this project was done via 2D visualization. In this final stage she moved from flat technical sketching to designing on actual figures. As a result, her designs slowly became more and more refined and she developed a better sense of what she was creating. Instead of erasing sketches that didn't work, she kept all sketches, well-designed or not, so that she could further understand what was and wasn't working and re-sketch the design to solve any outstanding issues.

She pasted key images of Goldsworthy's work all around the design sketches, wrote Post-it notes, made lists and reminders, along with words that she found relevant. Again, she was using a very systematic method of working, continuing in the linear vein in which she began.

This is a good example of process that remains consistent throughout. Andrea began in a very organized way, by collecting research and gathering images. Working mainly in a 2D visualization format, she created a narrative at each stage of her process.

Recognize emerging themes within design

Now that her concept was finalized, Andrea decided to translate it aesthetically in a number of ways. She utilized drawstrings for permanence and dramatic silhouettes, fragility and aggressiveness, all at the same time.

Cut-outs and drawstrings reinforced the idea of the permanence within slightly more masculine silhouettes. No overt sexiness was represented; the cut-outs served the purpose of achieving a fragile rather than a sexy look, utilizing athletic details within a natural colour palette. Comfort was key, while constantly taking into consideration the needs of a permanent, life-long garment.

A more 'off-the-body' silhouette with seaming details emerged. This allowed for more movement within the garments, and also allowed a mixture of textures and fabric piecing within the same garment to be used. Although this gave a slightly more catwalk appeal, the designs could also could easily be translated to ready-to-wear if worn individually and not as a whole look.

This flexibility and range of choice for the consumer is central to Andrea's thinking, and is something she always keeps in mind when designing. Worn together, her clothes have a more edgy catwalk appeal but bought individually, they translate well for a broader customer who is looking for a specific item.

1 / 2 / 3 / 4 / 5 / 6
Sketchbook pages

Andrea worked methodically through her sketchbook, sketching, editing streamlining and eventually ending up with key items in flat, black-and-white sketches.

Finalize design ideas, fabrication and details

In this final stage, it was important to Andrea to clearly define her customer and aesthetic. Clearly defined as a tomboyish woman, into athletic-inspired clothing and natural fibres, Andrea pictured her customer as being adventurous and with her own personal style. She imagined her to pay attention to trends and to buy from young designer or contemporary markets. But most importantly, Andrea perceived her customer to pay very close attention to detail: 'She wants to put on my clothing because it makes her feel comfortable and most like herself. The garments are an expression of how she feels or how she wants to feel. She has an urban sensibility, and a love for vintage and quirky things.'

Andrea created her own machine knits in earthy tones and developed 3D textural embroidery to further enhance the aesthetic and support the theme of the collection.

Following her previous process of designing 'piece by piece', Andrea finalized her key items in black-and-white flat sketches in order to see each piece clearly before styling them together into looks. This process works well for some designers who think of items within a collection as multiple parts forming the whole, but others work in reverse, envisioning the entire collection and overall theme in the abstract, working inwards towards the individual pieces themselves.

The colour palette was filled with autumnal yet bold colours in cotton, nylon, broadcloth, and corduroy with machine and hand-knits adding pattern and texture. Pops of red and pale chamois added dimension.

7 / 8
Final knitwear and embroidery swatches
The colour palette was autumnal, with bold accents and natural fibres.

Establish your voice, identity and signature style

Overall, Andrea's collections are colourful and print-oriented with an emphasis on layering and merchandising (the latter is crucial): 'Luxury items nowadays should embody the staples of each wardrobe. Perhaps the denim jacket is no longer the American staple; maybe this has been surpassed by the nylon hoodie with knit sleeves that detach and a drawstring waist. As a customer, I recognize its durability, its modernity, and the attention to detail in the design (and why it costs $400!). A sweater, pair of jeans, and a denim jacket are no longer staples in every wardrobe. If a collection is well merchandised, unique pieces that create emotion yet are wearable and accessible become the new staples.'

Andrea wanted to provide her customer with pieces that would have longevity. She sought to create desire for every piece because it tells the story of that season: 'My aesthetic is constantly developing, and with each failure and success in a collection, I am able to hone in more and more on my customer's identity. So much of my design philosophy is centred on attention to detail and an optimistic approach to clothing. Optimistic in the colour sense, the embellishments, the prints and textures, and in the way the wearer feels in the garments.'

She wrestles with the concept of 'luxury', does it reside in styling or fabrication – or both? Andrea's philosophy is centred on the fact that people pay for a feeling, and clothes create an expression of their personality and provide an opportunity to communicate who they are to the world.

Andrea believes that what women really need now (and the customer she designs for embodies this) are clothes that are comfortable and casual, filled with details and functionality in optimistic fabrics, colours, and prints. Embellishments give her casual garments an added value. She loves embroidery, beading, fabric manipulations and prints and handcrafted quality. She also feels a need to return to artisanal craft and attention to detail. This is why embellishments are key in her collections and she uses textures and knits because they create a sensory response: 'My collections are always focused on separates (tops, jackets, pants etc.). Again, it is about the wearer's wardrobe and the function it serves. Her jacket is perfect for a multitude of occasions, a garment that maximizes wearability. I also understand that dramatic pieces are important; so many of my clothes are runway-appropriate. This juxtaposition grew out of my love for the complicated and the dramatic. My clothes are styled in a complex manner, using layers of different garments to create cut-out shapes. For example, there are tiny peaks of a contrast placket underneath a semi-sheer vest, or a printed trouser worn with a printed top. It had been a struggle in the past to find a good middle ground between ready-to-wear and runway, and recently I was able to achieve this as many of my pieces can be more easily translated. Many of my design ideas just spit out onto the page and, as a result, my elaborate concepts might end up over-designed and unfocused – it is a long process to bring them back to a good balance between ready-to-wear and runway.'

9 / 10

Final illustrations

Andrea felt that her final collection successfully delivered what women need from their clothes: comfort, value and functionality, combined with detail, colour and print.

Turn to page 44 to see PART I (Idea) of this project, or page 108 for PART II (Concept).

Graphic imagery translated into three-dimensional silhouettes via innovative knitwear techniques.

Process

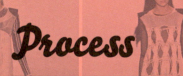

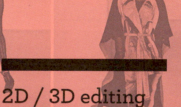

2D / 3D visualization

Photography

3D reconstruction

3D draping

3D shape / form

Idiom

2D editing

3D draping

2D sketching

Textile / knit development

2D visualization

Photography

Digital technology

Knit innovation

2D / 3D editing

3D sketching

3D knit / textile innovation

3D draping

3D construction

Colour / fabrication

Technical knit development

Editorial photography

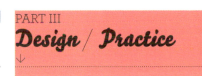

Trompe L'Oeil

Sara Bro-Jørgensen

On **pages 114–119**, we saw how Sara experimented with graphic shapes on the dress form, using a variety of different textiles and textures.

Reinvent new silhouettes and forms

This phase was first about evaluating what Sara had developed so far, and understanding why and where she would take it next, what to develop further and what to take out. She drew rough sketches of her design ideas, shapes and techniques.

Sara usually designs the textiles first and then finds the right silhouette for the specific textile. She develops the knit technique and then drapes on the dress form using the knitted sample to find the shape. For example, when developing the trench coats, she designed the fabric and didn't want to cut into the image so therefore had to make the shape very simple to showcase the image to its fullest potential: 'I think this is quite different from how most designers work as they tend to work on a silhouette and then find the right fabric for it.'

Sara then selected the sketches that worked for the collection. She selected those where the proportions, fabrics and shapes worked aesthetically and placed these together in a line-up. Then she entered into a long, focused sketching process, this time focusing on details. This included small things such as changing the placement of a pocket, moving the techniques on a knitted pattern around until she got it right or moving the silk tulle fringes up or down until they were in exactly the right place on the garment.

The collection line-up can change substantially at this final stage in the design process. In this case, the order dictated which looks Sara ended up choosing since all the silhouettes needed to work together on the catwalk; her goal was for the looks to be cohesive but neither too similar nor too different. This is a tricky balancing act that designers approach in a variety of ways. Some may elect to make a statement by sending duplicates in a variety of colours down a catwalk in succession, while others focus on a more merchandised approach with a variety of silhouettes that balance one another.

1
Sketches focusing on shape and proportion
Sara sketched to find a selection of designs that would work together as a collection. This meant matching shape, proportion and, later, detail.

2
An early toile fitting, in jersey
When the designs became full size and on the body, Sara could clearly see what did and didn't work.

3
Final toile fittings, in final fabrics
Sara's final collection showcased a raw and dark, yet feminine aesthetic, combining fine fabrics and heavier knit techniques.

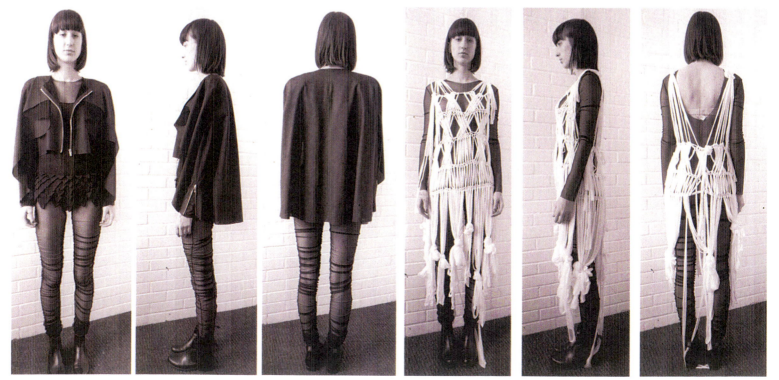

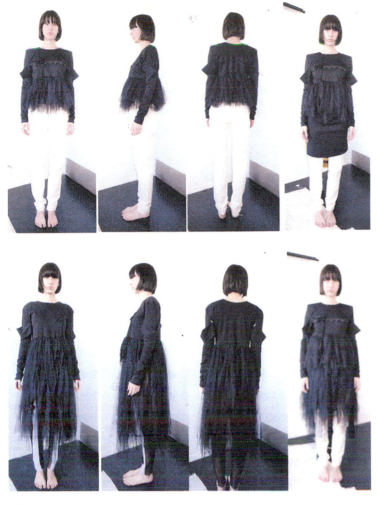

Recognize emerging themes within design

Sara selected the final designs and started making garments in muslin/calico prior to fabrication. When the designs became full size and she saw them on the body, everything changed. She could see clearly which ideas worked and which didn't, whether the proportions of a garment were right or not. In a drawing, scale can often look perfect but once transformed into life-size, it might look completely wrong and the proportions might need to be corrected.

When starting out, students often make the natural error of merely drawing, not designing, clothes. There is a huge distinction between the two and a reality check hits once a sketch goes through to the construction phase. It is easy to get caught up in the pose, the figure and the styling at the sketch stage and lose sight of the actual design, but the proportions of the body in reality impact this. Suddenly, what worked on the sketch doesn't work in reality, and adjustments have to be made.

Moving from sketch to actual garment development is an important stage, and speaks of the holistic nature of the design process itself; it is within the combined practice of both 2D and 3D (the space 'in between') that good design takes shape.

It is something of a myth that a designer sketches then makes exactly what they drew. Indeed, it is good to point out the difference between a designer and a technical pattern-maker or a sample-maker whose job is to interpret exactly what the designer has sketched. Within design development, this is not the goal; the sketch is merely the starting point – the first step on the journey towards discovering the evolution of the design in all its various incarnations.

Within her design journey, Sara travels back and forth between 2D visualization and 3D realization several times. At each step in this journey, she makes discoveries that inform the next step and lead to new conclusions. In this project, she entered into a rhythm of moving back and forth between 2D and 3D processes, sketching and toiling until she achieved the desired shape and proportion.

Finalize design ideas, fabrication and details

Sara's research from the photographs informed her colour palette of black and white and the selection of fabrics and yarns for the collection. She needed some very contrasting materials to represent her theme and chose a thin, silk tulle to recreate the light, dreamy feeling. It also had the right transparency, reminiscent of the light in the images. A thick, black, shiny silk yarn gave stable structure to her knitted pieces and blocked out larger areas of garments in order to create graphic knitted shapes such as the triangles. Leather was used to give a heavy, matte surface, as seen in some shadow areas in the photographs. Jacquards were knitted with Lycra to create tight bodysuits with graphic patterns, knitted and sized to fit the body.

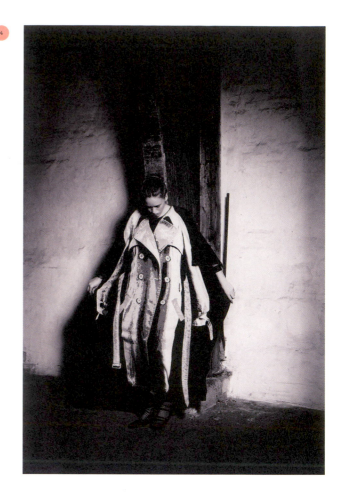

Establish your voice, identity and signature style

Sara describes her design aesthetic as raw and dark, yet feminine, with key detailing. This is exemplified through her boxy shapes and the often raw finishes on the garments, the graphic patterns and metal embroidery, the many layers and details, the delicate materials, and all the different knit techniques showcased together in each garment.

4 / 5 / 6 / 7 / 8

Final photo shoot

Her final photo shoot reinforced the black-and-white colour palette conceived in the earliest stages of the project.

Turn to page 50 to see PART I (Idea) of this project, or page 114 for PART II (Concept).

Experiments in new technology and materials.

Process

Social media research	3D draping	3D drape
2D photography	Textile development	Editing
2D flat pattern	Wearable technology	Collaboration
Repurposing	Fabric innovation	Textile development
Collaboration	3D construction	3D construction / innovation
	3D experimentation	Self-reflection
		2D collage

'Light Painting' by Leah Mendelson

185

PART I
Idea / Practice
56

PART II
Concept / Practice
120

PART III
Design / Practice
↓

Light Painting
Leah Mendelson

On pages 120–125, we saw how Leah evolved a 'foam' drape and incorporated the graphics from her photographs into drawings on the textiles and drapes.

Reinvent new silhouettes and forms

In this phase of the design process, Leah's challenge was to consider how she could 'drape' light, and how she could use this in her approach to silhouette. Her goal was to create completely original silhouettes and shapes that were outside an already established base of reality. Originality in her work is important and is driven by the desire not only to create something authentic, but different from her own expectations or preconceived notions. The key is experimentation: 'When something is original to me, it comes through discovery. It's something that I could not possibly conceive of when I started out designing. Original ideas arising from an experimental process are similar to the end of a story. You read a story not knowing what is coming next, but every word and chapter provides valuable information that leads to the conclusion. You don't start reading because you already know the end, you read because you don't and you want to find out. That's how I approach design; as an experiment and a story.'

In this instance, the silhouettes dictated by the light painting didn't follow any laws of physics. This was both a gift and a curse, as the process itself provided complete originality but the silhouettes were not based on reality nor did they relate to any existing methods of 3D draping in the traditional sense. Within the amorphous light painting silhouettes, there were infinite amounts of design solutions. With this project, Leah was challenged by an overwhelming amount of options. Editing was key. She realized this right from the start, during the initial photo shoot, when she knew that she had to find a design solution to salvage anything 3D and 'real' or 'physical' from the experiment.

The solution Leah chose out of the many possibilities was the one she liked best. It was also the last idea that she had come up with. She had experimented with several ways to design, all of which had failed to provide the best solution. Her search for perfection often created dissatisfaction, but she learnt a vital lesson throughout the process: nothing is wasted. The research and volume of work Leah undertook to explore the possibilities for this project contributed vastly to her learning and, as a result, fed several other projects.

When something is original to me, it comes through discovery. It's something I could not possibly conceive of when I started out designing. **Leah Mendelson**

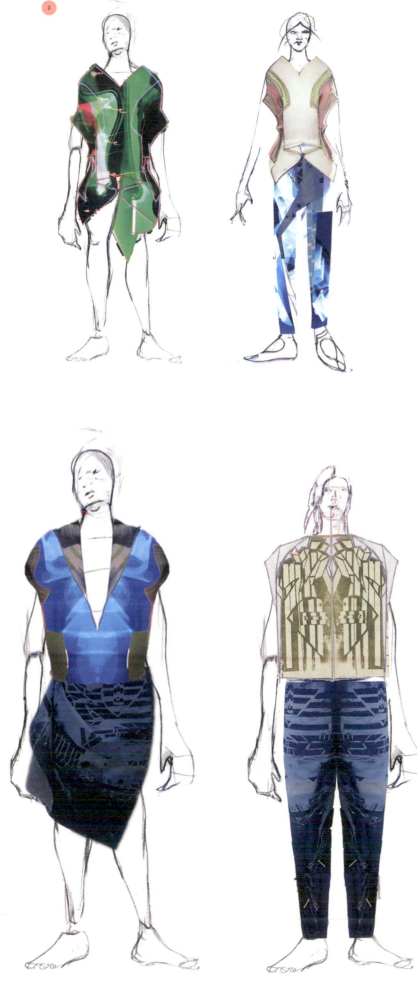

Recognize emerging themes within design

The constant in Leah's project was her emphasis on original pattern cutting techniques and textile development; both drove her design process forward. She also has great ability to draw on diverse sources of inspiration at the research stage, and this quality often presented itself in abstract forms. This project represents these processes well and clearly showcases Leah's open mindset, which lent itself so well to the act of discovery within any given process.

Finalize design ideas, fabrication and details

During this stage, Leah needed to focus on developing trousers/pant and skirts to pair with what were mostly tops from her 3D development stage. She liked the idea of working in denim and redefining the iconic pair of jeans. She again turned to textile development but had limited time and supplies. She decided to work with readily accessible household bleach and created her own stencils using scotch tape. She poured, dripped, and sprayed bleach over the denim through the stencils. She originally created several angular stencils, but soon discovered that the dripped, sprayed bleach created a more random pattern and made the denim look more organic. The shapes of the stencils were inspired by the angular method of applying the tape itself. She wanted a contrast to the curvy, organic shapes in the foam textile and also wanted the denim to have a 'harder, more street-wear' edge to contrast with the softness of the tops.

1 / 2

Final line-up

Leah used denim to counter the curvy, organic shapes of the foam textiles.

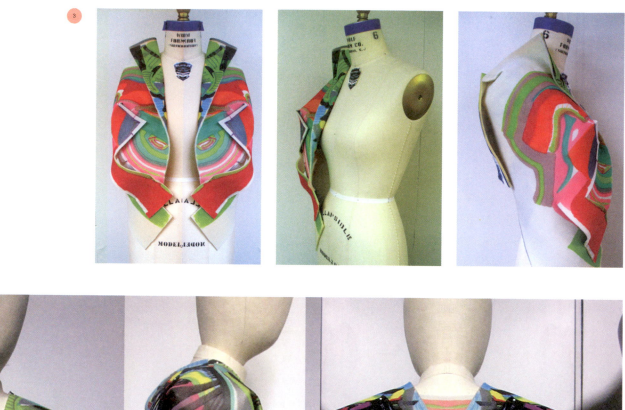

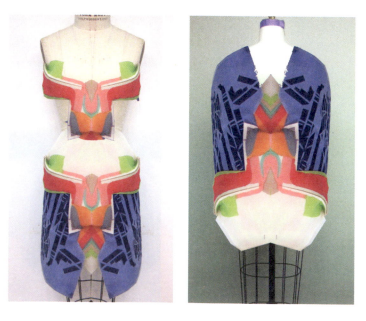

3 / 4 / 5 / 6
Final designs

Leah's final designs on the dress form. Her original photographs from the light painting shoot remained central to her theme throughout.

Establish your voice, identity and signature style

Leah usually tries to create original artwork by experimenting with an unfamiliar art form or medium. The spin-off projects provide her with different perspectives and processes. As noted previously, self-reflection is a valuable quality that emerging designers need to develop as much as their design skills. Knowing why you do something reveals the key to understanding your approach to design itself, and therefore enables more successful future development of ideas and concepts as you reflect on the themes within your work.

For Leah, the journey is just as important as the final result itself. In fact, because the journey is fully embraced it delivers the originality she seeks to produce.

This is a unique approach that fully embraces a random way of working in contrast to a more methodical linear approach. But the very personal nature of this method presents its own challenges: good editing skills are paramount. At the end of the day, designers need to deliver a product within a seasonal timeline. This is perhaps one of the biggest challenges for fashion designers: we not only produce art, but also need to meet the demands of the business of fashion, which are often unforgiving.

For Leah, this project revealed common threads within her approach to design: the projects she develops tend to be complex and very personal, no matter where she begins.

Her optimistic perspective on life is reflected in this approach to design: 'I think this optimism is a common quality among designers, and especially among fashion designers. Fashion reflects (and directs) society, and is constantly reinventing itself; it is the one of the most appropriate mediums for expressing the zeitgeist.'

6

Turn to page 56 to see PART I (Idea) of this project, or page 120 for PART II (Concept).

Soft, draped silhouettes, suspended away from the physical body.

Process

Visual research	3D innovation	**2D visualization**
2D visualization	2D sketching	**2D / 3D draping**
3D concepts	3D draping	**3D development**
Observational research	Materiality	**2D sketch line-up**
Narrative research	3D construction	**Editorial photography**
3D construction	3D tailoring	

Tensegrity

Aura Taylor

On pages 126–131, we saw how Aura played with different fabrics and suspension systems to try to find a solution for wearable garments.

Reinvent new silhouettes and forms

During this stage, Aura began finalizing concepts and ideas, translating them into concrete designs. After all the materials were sourced and concepts explored via 2D and 3D processes, she gathered all the visuals to sketch out the designs. She kept all the fabrics and trims in front of her as well as the research and 3D development pictures.

Her first attempts were based on the 3D lace structures that she had developed. From there, she directly sketched out the designs, but she soon found that this wasn't working – the results seemed too decorative.

Moving back to the tensegrity structure, Aura started draping in 3D, using the rayon jersey again. From this process, new silhouettes and garments were created on the dress form and Aura selected and edited from these for the final line-up.

1

Research wall
Aura kept all her fabrics, trims and research in front of her as she worked.

Recognize emerging themes within design

A key design detail that ran throughout the initial acupuncture collection was the idea of a metal and string structure that would hold the garment away from the body.

Aura cut a fine 1/8 inch diameter aluminium tubing and threaded it with satin silk cords to replace the simple sewing thread that she used for the initial experiment with the pins. (This is a great example of carrying over key elements from one project into another within a new context.)

This was used as a main design element and construction piece throughout the collection as well as the starting point for each garment. Several designs used perforated leather and strategically placed studs to imitate the acu-point patterns in the body, and the shapes and silhouettes were exaggerated in order to allow the lace to be built in different heights and levels. To complete the acupuncture line-up, Aura chose a monochromatic colour palette of black, white and silver to keep the focus on geometry and a graphic approach to represent the scientific data.

For Aura, it was key that her philosophy was reflected in the garment designs and in her presentation of her collection. The simple geometric squares and circles communicating the connections between the structure of the human body and other patterns in nature kept recurring and so she decided that this was something to reinforce in her presentation.

Fir this, Aura borrowed the symbolic language of Da Vinci's iconic 'Vitruvian Man'. This drawing is based on the correlations of ideal human proportions with geometry and Aura felt it was an appropriate visual graphic language to use to reinforce her concept:

'As I researched acupuncture maps and translated these into the geometric lace patterns, and as I looked further into other patterns in nature, I noticed amazing similarities between these scientific models. The Vitruvian Man summed up my entire research into a simplistic visual that I utilized to reinforce my own discoveries and present my designs.'

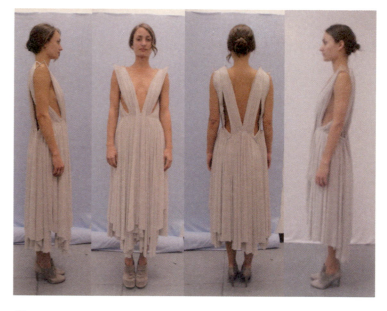

2

3

2 / 3
Realized garmenrs
Aluminium tubing and fine satin silk cords allowed Aura's designs to appear to be floating away from the body.

4 / 5 / 6
Presentation boards
For her presentation, Aura reflected the geometric shapes of Da Vinci's 'Vetruvian Man' to reflect the philosophy behind her designs.

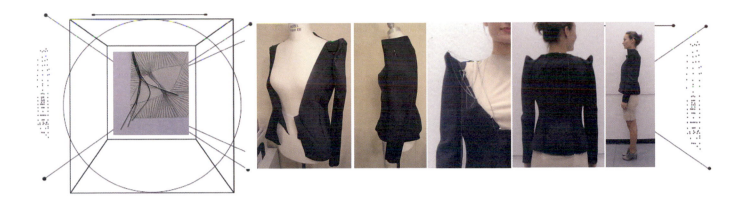

4

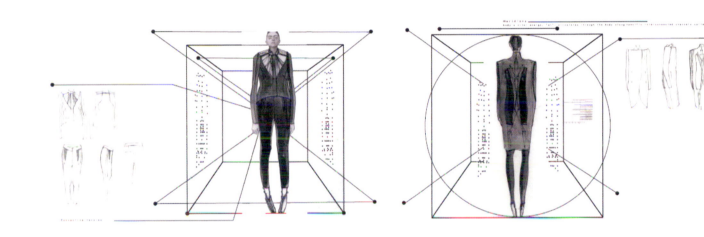

5

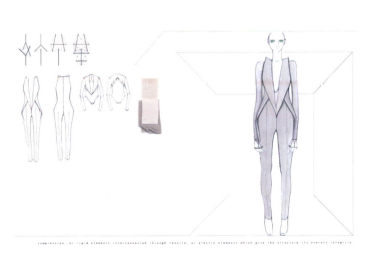

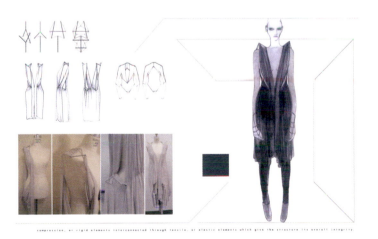

6

Finalize design ideas, fabrication and details

Although Aura kept the same aesthetic throughout the collection, her line-up highlighted simple shapes focusing on silhouettes and construction. She selected the most successful 3D drapes to design a cohesive collection, focussing on a minimal and architectural approach. She kept the exposed metal tubing structure as a construction piece and a main design element of the garments in the collection. In opposition to the fluid drapes created by stretch rayon jersey she introduced tailored pieces of wool and wool blends that mimicked the geometric pattern.

Aura's previous line up for the Acupuncture collection was based on one single idea where a range of looks/garments were designed to incorporate the 3D lace based on acu points in the body.

But Aura felt she was lacking her signature tailored aesthetic in the line-up so she worked to incorporate new shapes and structures that would represent this. The resulting line-up for Tensegrity was based on a balance between draped and tailored looks.

Establish your voice, identity and signature style

Aura describes her typical approach to design as one of in depth research and concept-driven design development within the process overall: 'Visual stimulus of an object or a thought followed by the development of a vocabulary and visual research will always be the driving force that creates meaning and thought behind each seam placement, logical representation and/or interpretation of an idea through silhouette. Because of this, my process varies each time based on the selected subject of interest that dictates the 2D or 3D development. This approach to design always challenges me to explore new territories and makes it so much more exciting. The Tensegrity collection resulted in the introduction of softer, draped silhouettes that were new to my aesthetic, however they were created in my own way by the solutions I found to achieve the look of garments suspended away from the physical body.'

7

7 / 8 / 9

Final line-up

Aura's final collection balanced the new draped designs with her signature tailored aesthetic.

Turn to page 62 to see PART I (Idea) of this project, or page 126 for PART II (Concept).

An investigation into shape-memory materials and new craft technologies and textiles.

Process

Investigation of craft

Data collection

Material / scientific research

Journaling

Material / scientific experimentation

Visual research

2D sketching

Fusion weaving

Fibre experimentation

Craft

Tradition and technology

Embroidery

Natural / artificial technology

Organic engineering

Natural programming

PART I	PART II	PART III
Idea / **Practice**	Concept / Practice	*Design* / *Practice*
68	132	↓

Techno Naturology

Elaine Ng Yan Ling

On pages 132–137, we saw how Elaine experimented with layering, laser-cutting, weaving and thermo-setting to investigate new textile possibilities.

Reinvent new silhouettes and forms

'Naturology' creates a living form, where interactive behaviour and the form itself become a reflection of their surroundings. Most importantly, the form is constantly evolving. 'Naturology' structures provide conditions that allow the design itself to create ever-evolving patterns, and, potentially, silhouettes. The transformation is created though the contrasting behaviour of the material, and the shape memory alloy that responds to the grain from the wood veneer. Although both of the materials respond to the constant change in time, they respond at different rates, allowing their behaviour to become symbiotic. Elaine's hybrid term, 'Naturology transformability' describes a distinct way to design: the form does not repeat itself and the behaviour of the form is synchronized with the change in temperature and humidity.

...fashion and form are intrinsically connected. **Elaine Ng Yan Ling**

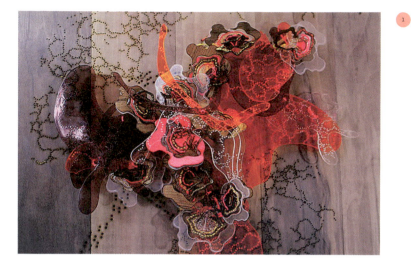

1

'The clusters'

A 'dancing rooftop' that moves when there is a source of energy, performing and changing to project different shadows. Each cluster contains different proportions of shape-memory material, allowing for unique responses and behaviours.

2

'The Flapper'

A fabric made up of a combination of cane, wool, polyester, wood and shape-memory polymer.

3

'Super LUX1'

A super-luxury intelligent fabric. The flaps connect to a circuit and change in reaction to the environment. The movement of the fabric creates an invisible spatial dialogue between people, space and fabric.

Recognize emerging themes within design

Elaine's concept is hugely influenced by the behaviour of the material. In order to create a hybrid material that can behave as if it lives by itself she decided to develop the concept into two design collections:

In the first, the design aimed to experiment and challenge the traditional ideas of shelter and to invite nature to take control within the development of architecture. This collection expresses the findings of Elaine's investigations into shape memory materials and the unpredictable behaviour of nature. It proposes how the hybrid shape memory tectonic system can be used on a large scale, for architectural purposes, under the premise that architectural design has no parameters. The collection is comprised of designs such as 'dancing rooftops', woven, flexible textiles and a super luxury, intelligent fabric.

The second collection explores the functional tectonic movement and behaviour of wood and turns it into a design to improve the daily experience of the user. The collection comprises designs such as 'dancing branches' and a flexible, woven material.

In terms of its application to fashion, it was interesting to note that if a garment is made from a shape memory material that is responsive to the human skin, it could, in theory, act as a second skin and allow the garment to sync with its silhouette.

4 / 5 / 6

Investigative illustrations

Illustrations exploring how malleable materials might be applied to become a human 'second skin'.

Finalize design ideas, fabrication and details

Elaine's hybrid material has been described as having a humanistic behaviour. This comment inspired Elaine to connect the concept of 'Naturology' within fashion as well as architecture.

Elaine comments, 'From my point of view, fashion is not merely restricted within the context of clothing. Fashion is also shelter. The perspective of seeing wood in its original state relates the Naturology concept to fashion. Fashion and architecture are rooted in the same concept: providing shelter and protection. In recent years architecture has been deriving shape and form from fashion tailoring, using fabric in the exterior of a building. In the past, fine artists such as Lucy Orter have been inspired by architecture and created fine art fashion pieces in the form of architecture. This shows fashion, architecture and form are intrinsically connected.'

Establish your voice, identity and signature style

Elaine's 'Techno Naturology' textile is the result of a unique combination of multiple materials, forming a bespoke architectural 'fabric' that delivers strength, flexibility, transformability and weather responsive systems. These qualities offer a tangible link between craft, architecture and engineering, taking a high-tech inspiration and combining it with what has been on offer for the past 1.5 billion years of evolution – the technology of nature.

The principles of Elaine's textile innovation can be widely applied and create natural connections between architecture and fashion. The impact of this advanced technology is yet to be seen but clearly Elaine is a pioneer leading us into the future of textile technology to be applied within the collective spheres of Architecture and Fashion.

A film of Elaine's work can be seen at: <http://vimeo.com/14522270>.

7

7

'Rewarding nature'

These pieces were made to be placed near to indoor plants. When the plants are watered, the pieces will dance and perform, implying a 'thank you', and creating an emotional attachment between the material and the user.

8 / 9

Motifs in movement

In many of Elaine's designs, mortifs come to life, as the material responds to its environment.

8

9

Turn to page 68 to see PART I (Idea) of this project, or page 132 for PART II (Concept).

Academic Perspective
Professor Frances Corner OBE
London College of Fashion

Have you seen a shift in the approach to design education regarding research, process and design?

I think the real shift has been to do with the developments in technology and social media. How fashion courses are taught is changing as staff not only integrate these aspects into their delivery but also as they require students to reflect on how technology has changed the design process, the nature of the fabrics and materials and how the goods and products are sold to the consumer. Staff use social media to enable groups of students to work online; staff and students collaborate on projects in ways that were inconceivable even five years ago; whilst the research process has been transformed through the use of the Internet. Nevertheless, at its heart the transformative nature of design education remains unchanged as each student learns how to integrate research, process and design into a personal view and vision.

Does this approach differ from country to country?

Yes I believe the approach does vary from country to country as the heritage, traditions, customs and beliefs inevitably affect the approach to both education and design.

Do you think good process is innate or can it be taught?

I believe that a good, thorough approach to the process of design can be taught and instilled in students. How each student individually interprets the process and how creative and original their response is can't in itself be taught but rather enhanced and developed.

Do you think there is a 'right' or 'wrong' way to design?

I don't believe there is a right or wrong way to design, because at the heart of any good design is the personal vision and view of the artist/designer, and it is impossible to say beforehand what is going to be original, creative and ultimately successful. Creative history is littered with examples of many great designers who have turned established ideas and traditions on their head. But how the concepts and ideas are developed and applied is where the need for careful thought about the process needs to take place. For something like fashion this is crucial; if you don't do it the right way the clothes won't hang together and the quality can't be guaranteed!

Can you share your thoughts on research in relation to student learning?

Research, and the subsequent experimentation and development of ideas, is central to the design process and the student learning experience. The process, aesthetics, identity and the reflection on what has been created all follow once the research and the experimentation has taken place. Encouraging the student to be expansive, inquisitive, curious, open-minded and challenging as they research and develop their ideas underpins the development of the student learning. Students need to come to understand the value of risk taking and making mistakes, that it is through these elements that they will learn how to push their ideas to the limit and that it is at this point that they will make the breakthrough necessary in the design process. Once students come to understand this and how it can be harnessed is a pivotal part in their creative and design development. Ultimately, this will ensure they will have a sustaining and sustainable design career.

Professor Frances Corner is Head of London College of Fashion, a role she has held since 2005. London College of Fashion is the only college in the UK to specialize in fashion education, research and consultancy. It offers a unique portfolio of courses that aim to reflect the breadth of opportunity available in the Fashion Industry. Prior Professor Corner held the position of Associate Dean in the faculty of Arts and Humanities at the University of Gloucestershire (1998 – 2001), and was Head of The Sir John Cass Department of Art, Media and Design at London Metropolitan University (2001 – 2005). Professor Corner trained as an artist, exhibiting widely, and then curated fine art exhibitions while also teaching foundation, degree and postgraduate course at Chelsea School of art and other institutions. She chaired the Council for Higher Education in Art and Design (CHEAD) until July 2009 and is a governing board member of the Fashion Retail Academy. As an expert in Art and Design Education, she is a writer and editor of Academic Studies, an advisor to the Department for Culture, Media and Sport on the Creative Economy, and a seasoned television interviewee.

Which is more important: commercial viability or creativity/vision?

I believe that creativity and vision is the most important element. As a student this has to be the paramount part of the learning process. Students need to understand the commercial and industrial context – it is not the vision without a reality check – but the vision has to be the starting point.

What are the most challenging aspects of design education today?

Keeping abreast of the latest developments in technology and how that affects teaching and learning, whilst at the same time keeping up with the changes in the industry, is particularly challenging. This is because institutions still need to teach traditional methods and processes. Judgments therefore have to be made as to how to balance these elements so the curriculum doesn't become too squeezed and the students learning disjointed.

How do we best prepare students for the global marketplace?

Having a web of strong international partnerships and relationships with academic institutions, industries and companies based in different countries is the most productive and helpful way of ensuring staff and students are aware of how the global fashion industry operates. This will help to ensure students are well prepared and able to have a fruitful and productive career within a complex, global industry.

Who, in your opinion, do you view as the most successful emerging young designers and what sets them apart?

As someone closely involved with the UK fashion education system, I view some of the UK young and emerging designers as playing a key role in the development of the global fashion industry. Not just because many UK fashion graduates go on to establish a successful profile and business of their own, but also because many work in the design teams of key international fashion houses. Designers such as Erdem, Christopher Kane, Richard Nicoll, Holly Fulton and Christopher Raeburn are all developing international profiles for their originality and freshness in their approach to fashion and I am watching their development with interest.

What advice would you give to a fashion design graduate/emerging designer seeking to establish their identity and aesthetic in today's global economy?

Work hard, keep focused, watch and listen to the industry around you – but keep true to your vision!

Designer Perspective
Gabi Asfour and Adi Gil
threeASFOUR

What is your design philosophy? How do you begin?

Gabi: Number one is collaboration, because we are a collaborative team. In addition to design we also run the business, take care of PR and sales and accounting – we are basically involved in every aspect of it fully. So I guess our philosophy, would be to know what you are doing from head to toe. I guess to do it our way.

What would your way be? What would that mean?

Adi: I think number one, what he said is about collaboration because we are three. And #2 I would say it is about the clothes. And the way we make clothes, the construction.

G: We've come up with a construction that is not classical construction. In order for us to do what we do, we have to know how to sew, how to pattern make, and also how to sell and market. We also have to know how to promote ourselves because we have a specific niche and message. We are learning as we go. This is another philosophy; that we can never really be completely satisfied. You need to always be open minded to even finding new ways within your ways. It's quite an interesting process because you always get excited. Because there's always some new thing happening and you're constantly responding to what's happening around you. And basically dealing with the unknown is exciting. It's very nerve-racking, but it's also exciting.

As your process has evolved has it been more instinctual or learned?

G: Instinctual, yes. We rely on our instincts in everything that we do. Including the business side.

How did the construction technique come about?

G: We basically realized that for us, the classical way of making clothes was not producing anything new. It might be producing something new for somebody else but for us it was not exciting enough. So we had to change the way we approached the construction of clothes. And of course, where you go is the anatomy of the human body. And the lines that exist on the human body are more beautiful than the lines that are used for constructing classical clothing. So we found that we could push the elegance and the beauty of the human body with seaming or constructing in a way that works with it, not against it. Maybe I shouldn't say against it perhaps but basically when you have these classical tailoring rules they sometimes cut the body in certain ways, like you get a knife and chop somebody up. So we felt that we could go around it.

A: We treat our clothes like sculpture, so for us it's a way of art. And we try to make them wearable at the same time. It's a nice challenge.

This New York City-based avant garde label was originally established in 1998 as ASFOUR, consisting of four designers: Gabi Asfour, Angela Donhauser, Adi Gil and Kai Khune. In 2001, the label won the Ecco Domani Fashion Grant given to innovative designers in the fashion industry. In 2005, Khune left the group to pursue his own label and the three remaining designers continued under the new title **threeASFOUR**. The experimental designs produced by threeASFOUR have been purchased and displayed by numerous prominent museums throughout the world including London's Victoria and Albert museum for the exhibit 'New York Fashion Now' and special exhibits at the Metropolitan Museum of Art (the 2005 exhibit 'Wild: Fashion Untamed' and the 2008 exhibit 'Superheroes: Fashion and Body'). The Costume Institute at Metropolitan Museum of Art has also acquired a several pieces for their permanent collection. Their works have also been featured in the Cooper Hewitt National Design Museum in New York, and Musee de la Mode et du Costume Galliera in Paris. ThreeASFOUR were also finalists in the Council of Fashion Designers of America and Vogue Magazine fashion fund award that is given to next generation of American fashion designers.

Within your process, as you create a collection, do you have a linear set of steps you go through or is it more random occurring as you feel driven?

G: It's both. It's a combination. We do have a set way in case we get too lost, but we like to open the doors for a bit of improvisation here and there. Because there's always excitement when it's a new way.

A: And it's three of us. So sometimes it takes longer, and you need to find a point in the middle somewhere.

Would you all start designing, draping, and then come together at certain points to talk about the collective ideas and move forward?

G: Yeah, something like that. The nice thing about fashion is you have deadlines. Deadlines are really important. We learned that deadlines force you to figure it out.

A: And stress you out!

If you were to look at your whole process, which of these words would you use to describe it? Literal, narrative, abstract, 2D visual, drawing, 3D sculpture on the dress form…

G: There's a little bit of everything. We leave it open.

A: Everyone brings something else to the table.

G: For the last collection, we had a lot of 2D sketches, because we had a lot of printed fabrics that we had to figure out the layouts. (You can see them on the boards) and a Parsons' student was interning with us. She is fantastic at sketching. So on Illustrator we are able to do a lot of flat, 2D development. But once the fabrics arrived that was not the case anymore, there was a need to prepare in 3D. But we usually start with an open playground. We don't know which way is going to be the beginning or the direction of the beginning.

A: But sometimes we know. This time we knew very well. This last collection we have been planning to do for over two years now so we knew exactly. And we do know on the next one also.

G: But yeah, 2D and 3D is how we start the process. Whenever it's a graphic thing, we start in two dimensions.

Do you brainstorm to talk about the theme?

G: Again, it's a more instinctual thing that you feel – and you know, 'This is it.' Sometimes ideas come and it takes a while for them to come about. But they're in the back of the head.

A: And sometimes it's just naturally that this is the next thing.

What are some of the strengths unique to each of you?

G: We have two females and one male. So the 'two verses one' opinion is a big advantage. We used to be four and then we had two verses two opinions, which wasn't always so good.

A: We got stuck with four.

G: Yes, we learned our lesson. We had the experience. So in the three-way relationship the 'two verses one' always solves the problem. It is an interesting process.

When you hit a wall (either individually or as a group) in your creative process what do you do?

A: Let it be. You have to take a moment and just let it be. I think it took a while to learn this. I think my personality is usually fighting and pushing, it's not just about making something. It's about a relationship of people. The older you are, you learn that and it's the same with making things. You have to let things be, because whatever is meant to be will be. I'm still learning. But I believe this is what you have to do.

G: See something else. For me it's more about switching to something else. I just take off, go away from fashion and do something else. Either you take a walk outside or take a walk on the wild side, or do construction, or make something else.

Is there a right or wrong way to approach design?

G: We don't believe in right and wrong.

A: You learn from mistakes.

G: Mistakes are necessary. There's no wrong way. You're always learning.

A: And if it wasn't right it probably happened for you to learn something. I look at it like that.

In relation to your process, how do you go about research?

A: We always research. We are Google freaks! We are very lucky to live at this time, because years ago we didn't have what we have these days. Research became easier, we can reach so much.

G: But the nice thing is you can do surface research, or you can really go in depth. And it's available. In-depth research is where you get the juice.

Experimentation is number one in the creative process. You need to be open to whatever is unknown to you. **Gabi Asfour**

Do you ever go on research trips or do you go places outside of the city to get inspired?

A: Trips happen. Obviously, they inspire us, but they were not planned solely for inspiration. Honestly, we get inspired by anything, just walking down the street.

Can you expand one what you said about surface vs. in depth research? Many students just Google search for images and information and don't go beyond that.

G: That's something I am against. Because I feel that in order to really know a subject you need to go really deep. Books are the best way to do that. But, you can do it on the Internet too, there's ways to go deeper into the research. And to get, like I said, 'the juice.' You won't get the juice from the surface. You just get the facade.

Can you give some examples of what you mean by that?

G: Analysis is key- where it came from and how it came about? One image is not enough, you need to have multiple images and from different places. So if it's an author on a subject, you need another author because you can't just act on one point of view. That's what's nice about the internet, you have access to who dealt with a certain subject and how they dealt with it and then you can get to the next one and the next one and you can differentiate and get some kind of outcome that is personal.

A: That's important too, making it personal. Just don't make it abstract research. It needs to become 'yours.' You need to take ownership of it and make it your own. Put it back out in the way that makes sense to you.

G: It needs to be individual and have an individual take on it, because then you can start to be original about it.

Could you explain your experimentation process?

G: Experimentation is number one in the creative process. You need to be open to whatever is unknown to you. Unknown – that's is the word that I use. Unknown territory is scary usually. Where you are not comfortable, you are not confident. But there is something driving you that goes beyond this, a certain kind of strength and a certain kind of faith in what you are doing that goes beyond the fear so you can overcome these fear barriers. We all like to be comfortable and like security, but that's not where the juice is.

Students are fighting against this all the time. It is very scary to be in that uncomfortable place and to not know.

A: And we chose to be like this, because we were never backed and we just went for it in order to do what we do. So our whole process is actually very scary. Our existence is scary, because we do not have a backer, so this is what we are dealing with everyday. The only thing I know is the sun is going to probably shine tomorrow and the moon is going to come at night, I don't know any more than that. For me, I have no securities.

None of us do, which is so ironic. We falsely think we have security in these things, but we don't. It's an illusion.

G: That's basically what we learned … this fake kind of security is an illusion.

A: I just know from our experience that we learned the hard way. And even the moon and the sun. I think they'll be here for a little bit, but I don't think they'll be here forever, for us. There is no guarantee.

Point of View

Colleen Sherin, Senior Fashion Director
Saks Fifth Avenue

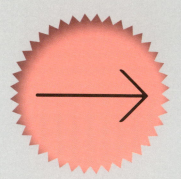

As Senior Fashion Director for Saks Fifth Avenue, **Colleen Sherin** travels the globe in search of trends, inspiration, and up-and-coming designers. Colleen covers the women's ready-to-wear collections in the world's fashion capitals of New York, London, Milan, and Paris and sets the tone for the trends the store will represent each season. She works closely with her merchants on fashion direction, direct mail catalogue imagery, and national ad campaigns.

Colleen has also explored the emerging fashion markets of Sao Paulo, Brazil, Sydney, Australia, and Lisbon, Portugal. As a champion of young designer talent, Colleen has discovered numerous collections for Saks Fifth Avenue.

She has appeared on national and local television programs and is quoted regularly in publications such as *Harper's Bazaar, Elle, InStyle, People,* the *Financial Times, The New York Times,* and *Women's Wear Daily* (WWD).

What do you look for when viewing a new collection?

When viewing a new collection, I look for innovative design, quality, and a product that the consumer will find desirable.

What does innovative design mean to you?

Innovative design is a creation that expresses a designer's distinct point of view.

Are there key elements you look for as a buyer?

When we are viewing a collection we're looking for ideas that are not duplicative of collections that we already have at Saks Fifth Avenue, we are looking for something that compliments or enhances the store's point of view. There is so much competition in the marketplace, that to stand out a designer really needs to have a distinct point of view and a unique offering. There isn't room for duplication anymore.

What makes a product desirable to a consumer?

It may be something that is so amazing, so exciting and so different that he/she just has to have to it. Whether or not he/she needs it. It's an emotional sort of thing. It may fill a void or a need or it may be just something that elicits such an emotional reaction that he/she has to have it. That's what creates desire.

Do you go with your gut instinct and just 'know' when you see it or are there tangible elements that are key?

It is business sense, but it is also important to have a gut reaction to something and go with that instinct. I think it is a combination of the two, you have to make thoughtful decisions that are prudent from a business point of view but they can't lack emotion entirely. You have to have a reaction to something - that is what gut instinct is.

Do you view the designer's process and approach to design as key in developing their vision, aesthetic and point of view as a designer? If so, please elaborate. Is research important? References to culture etc. ...

Many of today's most successful designers have their finger on the pulse and are tuned in to current and past cultural references (art, film, music, and literature) as well as taking inspiration from the street. It is about what is happening currently but also about being tuned in to interesting things that have happened in the past and can be reinterpreted. It is important to have respect for the past, but not to reference it too literally. If a designer is referencing a decade: the 20s, 30s, 40s or whatever it may be, it cannot be too literal because then it just looks like costume design. It still needs to have a modern, relevant, current spin to it.

Do you ever meet with emerging designers to give them guidance?

Yes, I preview collections a lot with designers and their teams prior to completion.

Does this process have an impact on the customer? Or is just a visceral reaction to good clothes?

In the end, for the consumer, items just need to translate into desirable designs that suit their lifestyle. I don't know that the consumer is getting so hung up on inspirations and references and I think in the end she wants a desirable product, something she has a connection to. Increasingly we are finding that the consumer is looking for longevity, something that she can buy and wear for years to come. She is also looking for versatility; pieces she can wear many different ways, for quality and price-value relationship. In the past few years we have seen a shift at retail, the consumer has been more thoughtful before making a purchase and is considering all these factors.

What makes a design 'good'?

Good design is timeless – for example, good design from the 1920s, 30s or 50s still feels relevant now. Good design transcends the decades.

What is that magic bullet that makes some items stand out over others?

Sometimes there is that sort of magical moment when viewing a collection where there is this item that is so perfect that it becomes a "must have" item of the season. Then it can become iconic or a collectable piece. That does happen. All of the design elements align and it is just right for that particular moment.

What elements do you see as key in the development of a young designer?

Drive, ambition, energy, imagination, creativity balanced with business sense.

How can designers balance this?

As a designer it is important to be creative and again it goes back to that idea of trying to do something that hasn't been done before, or doing something in a different way so that you fill a void or a need and don't duplicate something that has already been done. With that said it needs to be tempered, it still needs to be something that is commercially viable. In the end you want the consumer to buy and to wear what you are designing. So I think it is a balance between the creativity and the reality of the business that we're in.

Would you advise young designers starting up to find a business partner that could be the Yin to their Yang? Can designers succeed without this?

I think that is why you see these pairings, because they play off one another. They each have their strengths that they bring to the table, and I think that can be very helpful. I think if a designer does not have those skills on their own, to partner with somebody who does and who understands the design aesthetic they are trying to achieve and can balance it with business sense would be very helpful. It's hard for a young designer because they may not have the budget for this and they may have to wear all the hats at once. But ideally you should have someone to collaborate with in this role.

What's more important, commercial viability or creativity? Or is a marriage of both desirable?

They are equally important. One cannot survive without the other.

Should we be teaching equal parts business and design in art/design schools to better prepare emerging designers?

I don't know that it has to be 50/50 but I do think that the business element should be in the curriculum, certainly. I don't think you want to detract from the creative or technical training that a young designer needs. But I do think they need to be educated about the business side of fashion if they are going to succeed and have a viable career.

What advise would you give to a fashion design graduate entering today's global marketplace?

Create a product that fills a void and elicits an emotional response from the consumer. Create desire. That is part of the magic of design.

What do you think the difference is between creating fashion and designing clothes?

I think students have to dream and they have to think out of the box and take risks - calculated risks. And then they should bounce those ideas off either a business partner or someone they are collaborating with. It's very common for big design houses to have commercial or merchandising teams to work with the design team to develop their designs and review them together. It becomes a compromise in terms of producing the end product that's going to be delivered to the consumer. It starts with the designer's vision but the merchandising is an important step.

As design students, if there was a time in their life when they are going to have an opportunity to experiment it's now. I would highly encourage that within the curriculum they are allowed to dream and take risks and in order to be ultra creative, but to also understand that in the real world some of those designs may be modified to make them commercially viable and to understand that this is part of the process. I don't think they should be discouraged from generating these creative 'editorial' ideas now, because this is their time to experiment and I think that is really important.

Appendix

Glossary
Further Resources
Index
Acknowledgements

Glossary

2D collage: A method of utilizing photography or existing imagery of 3D processes to create two-dimensional figures or illustrations of looks or garments.

2D final presentation: A two-dimensional layout showcasing the final edited selection of best looks from the collection; often including mood/fabric board along with illustrations/collage and flat technical sketches.

2D sketching: Drawings in any two-dimensional media, via hand or computer.

2D sketch line-up: Sketched figures arranged in a linear form representing the final edited collection of looks

2D styling: A method of visualizing looks two-dimensionally on the body/figure prior to entering the 3D process and can be created via collage, sketches or digitally manipulated figures. This tool can be used to explore particular illustration styles or how items/garments are worn on the figure in two-dimensional media.

2D/3D draping: Physically arranging fabric and/or the representation of arranged fabric, such as fabric on a dress form or a photo of fabric on a dress form.

2D visualization: A mental image, concept or visual perception that is first translated via two-dimensional media. Can include images, photographs and sketches.

2D visual merchandising: The act of editing designs throughout the design process in order to streamline head-to-toe looks, colour and fabrication.

3D concepts: An abstract idea drawn from or brought into a three-dimensional form via draping.

3D construction: The physical assembly of a design idea via cutting/sewing techniques.

3D digital draping: A method of draping fabric via 3D software or simply by scanning 3D draped from the form into a digital program for further manipulation.

3D innovation: Creating new methods, designs, ideas or products in three-dimensional form.

3D tailoring: A three-dimensional garment construction technique leading to the creation of a structured garment using woven (non-knit) fabrics.

3D visualization: A mental image, concept or visual perception that is first translated via three-dimensional means (draping/pattern-drafting etc.).

Airdye® printing technology: AirDye is a revolutionary new way to dye and print fabric without using water. AirDye® technology features a one-step process that bypasses the liquid state of dye altogether. Proprietary dyes are transferred from paper onto fabric using heat – without consuming water or emitting pollutants. The entire process is waste-free: the paper is recycled, and used dyes and toners are also recycled to make tar and asphalt. Using AirDye® to print or dye a single garment can save up to 25 gallons of water. *http://fashion.airdye.com/what/*

Arduino platform: Arduino is an open-source electronics prototyping platform based on flexible, easy-to-use hardware and software. It's intended for artists, designers, hobbyists, and anyone interested in creating interactive objects or environments.

Biomimicry: Refers to mimicking the behaviour and engineering of nature. The natural responsive system is nature's way of responding to its surroundings, within which biomimicry has become a very influential phenomenon, particularly in recent years and within the field of functional design.

'Blistering': This technique makes the image appear softer and less graphic. Done on a digital knitting machine the blistering technique is knitted in two layers in some areas and single in others thereby creating this effect.

Brainstorming: Lists of ideas gathered spontaneously, used in creative problem solving around a central theme. It can be done individually, but more effectively in groups.

Cortical growth: A neurological term relating to the growth of the cerebral cortex.

'Craftnology': A hybrid word invented by Elaine Yang Ling Ng, combining craft and technology.

Customization of details: A process of specifically designing the details within garments themselves such as: Hardware, trims, stitching, buttons, zippers etc.

Customer profile: An outline or concept of the ideal customer that matches your aesthetic, design sensibility or brand identity. This can include lifestyle choices such as: career, marital status, and personal preferences along with similar brands he/she would wear.

Designing 'piece-by-piece': This term was coined by Andrea Tsao to describe her process of design whereby she sketches each garment separately then builds head-to-toe looks then collections from this starting point.

Design language: An expression or grouping of words that has a figurative meaning in the context of design; creating a unique expression or language.

Digital technology: Computer-aided software and hardware used in the creation of design related activities. Primarily inclusive of the Adobe suite: Photoshop, Illustrator and InDesign in combination with digital devices such as smart phones, Ipads, MP3 players, Wacom tablets etc.

Editorial direction: Specific instruction given (either within a 2D process or photographic shoot) in order to achieve a desired artistic result or outcome.

Elasticity (physics): continuum mechanics of bodies that deform reversibly under stress.

Ethics: A moral philosophy involving defending and recommending a set of concepts of right and wrong behaviour. Within the context of this text, this often refers to issues surrounding establishing sustainable practice within the fashion industry.

Fabric manipulation: A process including pleating, folding, appliqué, layering, gathering, trapunto and a myriad of other techniques to create innovative design solutions.

Fashion cultural reference: Specific cultural references related to existing trends within the fashion industry representing the 'trickle-down' effect of ideas from designer to the high-street.

Flat-sketching: A technical method of drawing garments proportionally showing front, back, side views along with close-ups of collars, sleeves or other key details. This tool is typically used to communicate garment construction to patternmakers prior to cutting fabric to make the garment. It can be hand-drawn or digitally created.

Fusion weaving: A term invented by Elaine Yang Ling Ng to describe the process of developing the textile itself.

Humid reactive: Fibres that respond to a change in humidity.

Hybrid materialization: Forming composites that consist of two or more constituents at the molecular level.

Hybrid tectonic system: An intelligent kinetic system that can be achieved through mimicking the responsive systems of both artificial and natural sensors, and an approach for utilizing technology to create architectural structures that address a dynamic, flexible and constantly changing demand. Responsive structures are those that measure actual environmental conditions to enable buildings to adapt their form, shape, colour or character responsively, and can be refined and extended to improve the perception of spatial experience and challenge the definition of what a shelter is.

Journaling: A personal record of thoughts, experiences and reflections surrounding a particular topic or theme. This is a regular practice similar to a Diary and is useful within the design process.

Knit innovation: The act of creating new knit stitches and techniques.

Light photography: This is a cross between the medium of film and photography, capturing time passing as a still photograph. It is a simple photographic technique whereby you move a source of light in a darkened room with the camera's shutter open for longer than usual. By doing so the camera records the movement of the light source as a passage of time.

Materiality: The quality of being material or of matter; in the context of fashion pertaining to innovations in fabrication.

Mind mapping: A visual diagram used to capture information and ideas. It is often created around a single word or text placed centrally, from which related ideas, words and concepts are drawn. It can be created via a number of ways with written notes or visual sketches, photographs or mixed media. Major categories emerge directly from the starting point with sub-categories of themes branching out from these.

Narrative research: The systematic investigation and study of all materials related to stories or other literary materials.

Natural programming: Creating a system that is easier to learn and use.

Naturology: A hybrid word that combines nature and technology.

Observational research: The systematic investigation and study of all materials through the act of watching carefully and attentively.

Organic engineering: Organic, hydroponic, aeroponic or aquaponic technologies designed as an engineering system.

Programmable micro-controllers: Another commonly used term is Programmable Interface Controller, or PIC micro-controller. PIC's are electronic circuits that can be programmed to perform a vast range of tasks.

Re-purposing: The practice of re-using a material, object or item for a new purpose.

Self-reflection/Self-editing: A method of stopping within your process to evaluate work done thus far, assessing decisions that have been made and asking critical questions before moving forward in a considered manner.

Shape memory alloy (SMA): Considered as a functional material. The attractive potential of SMA includes its reversible strains of several percent, generation of high recovery stresses and the ability to lift a heavy weight. Most industrial applications of SMA have been used for on/off applications, such as cooling circuit valves, fire detection systems, clamming devices. SMA is very popular as an actuator, as the motor actuator can be reduced to a single SMA wire. The wire replaces all the complicated motor systems, is more compact and reliable and due to the absence of the electrical component, the shape memory actuator become a silent, friction-reduced and spark-free device.

Shape memory materials: Matter or element having the ability to return from a deformed state to their original state.

Smart materials and technologies: Designed materials and technologies having one or more property that changes in a controlled fashion by external stimuli, such as stress, temperature, electric or magnetic fields, and pH.

Space appropriation: A term created by Melitta Baumeister to describe the act of making a public space or environment your own and imprinting it with your vision.

Symbiotic: Dissimilar organisms, ideas, concepts, or visualizations living together.

Technical drawing: A method of mapping out technical details (stitches, construction, print repeats etc.) via computer-aided software.

Techno naturology: This structure carefully considers the proportional relationship between the wood veneer and the shape memory alloy /polymers. The growth is studied within a confined space such as the growth of deformed tree roots and neurons within the brain. These structures allow the material to support itself, as well as to flexibly transform with reduced friction when in action.

Tectonic movement: Using artificial technology to activate and stimulate nature's technology in order to create tectonic movement. The vision of 'Naturology' tectonic movement is not just about mimicking the behaviour of nature but adding a sense of fluidity and functional responsiveness to the architecture, facilitating it to complement and harmonize with its environment.

Thermo reactive: Fibres that respond to change in temperature.

Two-colour jacquard: A knitwear technique knitted on a digital knitting machine in only one layer using two different colour yarns resulting in a two-colour graphic effect.

Visual research: The systematic investigation and study of all materials that stimulate the optic sense, such as videos, pictures, photographs, illustrations, etc.

Wearable technology: Clothing and accessories that incorporate computer and advanced electronic technologies. Designs often incorporate practical functions and features, but may also have a purely critical or aesthetic agenda.

Zero-waste pattern cutting: As the term suggests, this is a method of constructing and cutting garments without wasting any fabric. The designer approaches the design process from this standpoint.

Further Resources

Books on design

Basics Fashion Design 01: Research and Design by Simon Seivewright, 2007, AVA Publishing.

Drape Drape by Hisako Sato, 2012, Laurence King.

Drawing on the Right Side of the Brain | by Betty Thomas, 2001, Harper Collins.

Fashion Designers' Sketchbooks by Hywel Davies, 2010, Laurence King.

Fashion: The Century of the Designers 1900–1999 by Charlotte Seelig, 2000, Konemann.

Isabel Toldeo: Fashion from the Inside Out by Valerie Steele and Patricia Mears, 2009, Yale University Press.

It's Not How Good You Are, It's How Good You Want To Be by Paul Arden, 2003, Phaidon Press.

Maison Martin Margiela: 20: The Exhibition by Bob Verhelst and Kaat Debo, 2008, MoMu.

Pattern Magic by Tomoko Nakamichi, 2012, Laurence King.

Rei Kawakubo: ReFusing Fashion by Harold Koda, Sylvia Lavin, Judith Thurman, 2008, MOCAD (Museum of Contemporary Art, Detroit).

Skin + Bones, Parallel Practices in Fashion and Architecture by Brooke Hodge, Patricia Mears and Susan Sidlauskas, 2006, Thames & Hudson.

The Design Process by Karl Aspelund, 2006, Fairchild Books.

The Fundamentals of Fashion Design by Richard Sorger and Jenny Udale, 2007, AVA Publishing.

The Warhol Economy How Fashion & Art Drive New York City by Elizabeth Currid, 2008, Princeton University Press.

Visual Research Methods in Fashion by Julia Gaimster, 2011, Berg Publishing.

Visualizing Research, A Guide to The Research Process in Art And Design by Carole Gray and Julian Malins, 2004, Ashgate Publishing Ltd.

Concept stores

A special mix of brands and products identifies a 'Concept store'. It's a modern experience of shopping, always in motion and highly innovative. The store addresses particular groups of customers: e.g., luxury, design and street-wear customers. The range of products and brands are wide and some stores change the floor layout and products regularly to stay flexible and surprising.

Antwerp
http://www.clinicantwerp.com

Berlin
www.andreasmurkudis.com
http://xxx-berlin.com

London
www.doverstreetmarket.com

Los Angeles
www.mossonline.com

Milan
www.10corsocomo.com

New York
www.grandopening.org
www.mossonline.com

Paris
www.colette.fr

San Francisco
www.harputsmarket.com

Tokyo
www.openingceremony.us/about/tokyo.html

Websites/Blogs

Design Milk
http://design-milk.com

Ecouterre
www.ecouterre.com
(sustainablity)

Edelkoort
www.edelkoort.com/trendtablet
(visionary forecasting)

Fashionary
http://fashionary.org/blog

Final Fashion by Danielle Meder
http://finalfashion.ca

Outsapop by Outi Pyy
www.outsapop.com (a good resource for those who design through making)

New Museum
www.newmuseum.org
(New York museum)

Slow Retail
http://slowretailen.wordpress.com
(interesting retail concepts)

The Creator's Project
http://thecreatorsproject.com (inspiring, cutting edge innovation and technology)

Trend Land
http://trendland.com (cool updates on art/design objects)

Magazines and Publications

A Magazine Curated by Martine Sitbon
Another Magazine
Bloom
Dazed and Confused
Elle
Encens
Harpers Bazaar
I-D
Interview
Numero
Nylon
Paper
Ponytail
Surface
Textile View
V
Viewpoint
Visionaire
Vogue
Wallpaper
Women's Wear Daily (WWD)

International Fashion Competitions

Arts of fashion
http://www.arts-of-fashion.org

HYERES
http://www.villanoailles-hyeres.com

ITS International Talent Support
http://www.itsweb.org

MITTELMODA
http://www.mittelmoda.com

Index

Acknowledgements

This book is the result of cumulative knowledge from my twenty-three years working in the fashion industry, eight years of teaching practice, and endless hours sitting in front of students figuring out how to guide them through their process. So many experiences and people throughout the years have contributed to my abilities, and encouraged me towards the thoughts that eventually formed this text.

During my years at Parsons The New School For Design and indeed in life, I have always reached beyond my grasp, and have been stretched to grow and challenge myself personally, professionally and academically.

I could not have completed this book without the help of my wonderful research assistants - Jovana Mirabile and Mary Beth Bachand, who put in ceaseless hours transcribing interviews, uploading images and generally keeping me on track!

Many thanks to all the contributors who agreed to participate and who patiently went back and forth with multiple edits before we finalized the content and images. Thank you for unmasking your process to enable others to learn from it.

To Shelley Fox, who so graciously agreed to write the foreword to this book.

Thank you also to John Hopkins, Van Dyk Lewis and Hilary Hollingworth for help with reviews of early content.

To Caroline Walmsley from AVA Publishing who believed in the concept from the beginning and to my editor, Leafy Cummins for the innumerable hours spent bringing this book to life.

To Mum, who sacrificed her dreams so that I could realize mine. To Dad, who always believed in everything I could become.

Lastly, to my incredible soul mate and husband, Mark. Words cannot express my gratitude for your partnership in everything I do. Your invaluable feedback and editing made the text richer and more comprehensible.

To God be all the Glory.

Publisher's note

The subject of ethics is not new, yet its consideration within the applied visual arts is perhaps not as prevalent as it might be. Our aim here is to help a new generation of students, educators and practitioners find a methodology for structuring their thoughts and reflections in this vital area.

AVA Publishing hopes that these **Working with ethics** pages provide a platform for consideration and a flexible method for incorporating ethical concerns in the work of educators, students and professionals. Our approach consists of four parts:

The **introduction** is intended to be an accessible snapshot of the ethical landscape, both in terms of historical development and current dominant themes.

A selection of **further reading** for you to consider areas of particular interest in more detail.

The **framework** positions ethical consideration into four areas and poses questions about the practical implications that might occur. Marking your response to each of these questions on the scale shown will allow your reactions to be further explored by comparison.

The **case study** sets out a real project and then poses some ethical questions for further consideration. This is a focus point for a debate rather than a critical analysis so there are no predetermined right or wrong answers.

Required Reading Range
Working with ethics

Lynne Elvins
Naomi Goulder

Ethical: aware-
ness/
reflect-
ion/
debate

Introduction

Ethics is a complex subject that interlaces the idea of responsibilities to society with a wide range of considerations relevant to the character and happiness of the individual. It concerns virtues of compassion, loyalty and strength, but also of confidence, imagination, humour and optimism. As introduced in ancient Greek philosophy, the fundamental ethical question is: *what should I do?* How we might pursue a 'good' life not only raises moral concerns about the effects of our actions on others, but also personal concerns about our own integrity.

In modern times the most important and controversial questions in ethics have been the moral ones. With growing populations and improvements in mobility and communications, it is not surprising that considerations about how to structure our lives together on the planet should come to the forefront. For visual artists and communicators, it should be no surprise that these considerations will enter into the creative process.

Some ethical considerations are already enshrined in government laws and regulations or in professional codes of conduct. For example, plagiarism and breaches of confidentiality can be punishable offences. Legislation in various nations makes it unlawful to exclude people with disabilities from accessing information or spaces. The trade of ivory as a material has been banned in many countries. In these cases, a clear line has been drawn under what is unacceptable.

But most ethical matters remain open to debate, among experts and lay-people alike, and in the end we have to make our own choices on the basis of our own guiding principles or values. Is it more ethical to work for a charity than for a commercial company? Is it unethical to create something that others find ugly or offensive?

Specific questions such as these may lead to other questions that are more abstract. For example, is it only effects on humans (and what they care about) that are important, or might effects on the natural world require attention too?

Is promoting ethical consequences justified even when it requires ethical sacrifices along the way? Must there be a single unifying theory of ethics (such as the Utilitarian thesis that the right course of action is always the one that leads to the greatest happiness of the greatest number), or might there always be many different ethical values that pull a person in various directions?

As we enter into ethical debate and engage with these dilemmas on a personal and professional level, we may change our views or change our view of others. The real test though is whether, as we reflect on these matters, we change the way we act as well as the way we think. Socrates, the 'father' of philosophy, proposed that people will naturally do 'good' if they know what is right. But this point might only lead us to yet another question: *how do we know what is right?*

Further reading

AIGA
Design Business and Ethics
2007, AIGA

Eaton, Marcia Muelder
Aesthetics and the Good Life
1989, Associated University Press

Ellison, David
*Ethics and Aesthetics in European Modernist Literature:
From the Sublime to the Uncanny*
2001, Cambridge University Press

Fenner, David E W (Ed)
*Ethics and the Arts:
An Anthology*
1995, Garland Reference Library of Social Science

Gini, Al and Marcoux, Alexei M
Case Studies in Business Ethics
2005, Prentice Hall

McDonough, William and Braungart, Michael
*Cradle to Cradle:
Remaking the Way We Make Things*
2002, North Point Press

Papanek, Victor
*Design for the Real World:
Making to Measure*
1972, Thames & Hudson

United Nations Global Compact
The Ten Principles
www.unglobalcompact.org/AboutTheGC/
TheTenPrinciples/index.html

A framework for ethics

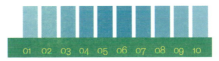

Your specifications
What are the impacts of your materials?

In relatively recent times, we are learning that many natural materials are in short supply. At the same time, we are increasingly aware that some man-made materials can have harmful, long-term effects on people or the planet. How much do you know about the materials that you use? Do you know where they come from, how far they travel and under what conditions they are obtained? When your creation is no longer needed, will it be easy and safe to recycle? Will it disappear without a trace? Are these considerations your responsibility or are they out of your hands?

Using the scale, mark how ethical your material choices are.

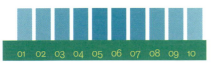

You
What are your ethical beliefs?

Central to everything you do will be your attitude to people and issues around you. For some people, their ethics are an active part of the decisions they make every day as a consumer, a voter or a working professional. Others may think about ethics very little and yet this does not automatically make them unethical. Personal beliefs, lifestyle, politics, nationality, religion, gender, class or education can all influence your ethical viewpoint.

Using the scale, where would you place yourself? What do you take into account to make your decision? Compare results with your friends or colleagues.

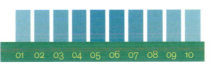

Your creation
What is the purpose of your work?

Between you, your colleagues and an agreed brief, what will your creation achieve? What purpose will it have in society and will it make a positive contribution? Should your work result in more than commercial success or industry awards? Might your creation help save lives, educate, protect or inspire? Form and function are two established aspects of judging a creation, but there is little consensus on the obligations of visual artists and communicators toward society, or the role they might have in solving social or environmental problems. If you want recognition for being the creator, how responsible are you for what you create and where might that responsibility end?

Using the scale, mark how ethical the purpose of your work is.

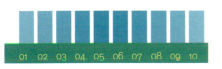

Your client
What are your terms?

Working relationships are central to whether ethics can be embedded into a project, and your conduct on a day-to-day basis is a demonstration of your professional ethics. The decision with the biggest impact is whom you choose to work with in the first place. Cigarette companies or arms traders are often-cited examples when talking about where a line might be drawn, but rarely are real situations so extreme. At what point might you turn down a project on ethical grounds and how much does the reality of having to earn a living affect your ability to choose?

Using the scale, where would you place a project? How does this compare to your personal ethical level?

Case study

One aspect of fashion design that raises an ethical dilemma is the way that clothes production has changed in terms of the speed of delivery of products and the now international chain of suppliers. 'Fast fashion' gives shoppers the latest styles sometimes just weeks after they first appeared on the catwalk, at prices that mean they can wear an outfit once or twice and then replace it. Due to lower labour costs in poorer countries, the vast majority of Western clothes are made in Asia, Africa, South America or Eastern Europe in potentially hostile and sometimes inhumane working conditions. It can be common for one piece of clothing to be made up of components from five or more countries, often thousands of miles apart, before they end up in the high-street store. How much responsibility should a fashion designer have in this situation if manufacture is controlled by retailers and demand is driven by consumers? Even if designers wish to minimize the social impact of fashion, what might they most usefully do?

Is it more ethical to create clothing for the masses rather than for a few high-ranking individuals?

Is it unethical to kill animals to make garments?

Would you design and make a feather cape?

Fashion is a form of ugliness so intolerable that we have to alter it every six months.

Oscar Wilde

Feather capes

Traditional Hawaiian feather capes (called 'Ahu'ula) were made from thousands of tiny bird feathers and were an essential part of aristocratic regalia. Initially they were red ('Ahu'ula literally means 'red garment') but yellow feathers, being especially rare, became more highly prized and were introduced to the patterning.

The significance of the patterns, as well as their exact age or place of manufacture is largely unknown, despite great interest in their provenance in more recent times. Hawaii was visited in 1778 by English explorer Captain James Cook and feather capes were amongst the objects taken back to Britain.

The basic patterns are thought to reflect gods or ancestral spirits, family connections and an individual's rank or position in society. The base layer for these garments is a fibre net, with the surface made up of bundles of feathers tied to the net in overlapping rows. Red feathers came from the 'i'iwi or the 'apapane. Yellow feathers came from a black bird with yellow tufts under each wing called 'oo'oo, or a mamo with yellow feathers above and below the tail.

Thousands of feathers were used to make a single cape for a high chief (the feather cape of King Kamehameha the Great is said to have been made from the feathers of around 80,000 birds). Only the highest-ranking chiefs had the resources to acquire enough feathers for a full-length cape, whereas most chiefs wore shorter ones which came to the elbow.

The demand for these feathers was so great that they acquired commercial value and provided a full-time job for professional feather-hunters. These fowlers studied the birds and caught them with nets or with bird lime smeared on branches. As both the 'i'iwi and 'apapane were covered with red feathers, the birds were killed and skinned. Other birds were captured at the beginning of the moulting season, when the yellow display feathers were loose and easily removed without damaging the birds.

The royal family of Hawaii eventually abandoned the feather cape as the regalia of rank in favour of military and naval uniforms decorated with braid and gold. The 'oo'oo and the mamo became extinct through the destruction of their forest feeding grounds and imported bird diseases. Silver and gold replaced red and yellow feathers as traded currency and the manufacture of feather capes became a largely forgotten art.